AF539702

Technical Education

DPH Education Series

Technical Education

U K SINGH • K N SUDARSHAN

DISCOVERY PUBLISHING HOUSE
NEW DELHI-110002

Reprinted - 2019

First Published - 1996

ISBN: 978-81-7141-355-3

Technical Education

Published by:

DISCOVERY PUBLISHING HOUSE PVT. LTD.
4383/4B, Ansari Road, Darya Ganj
New Delhi-110 002 (India)
Phone: +91-11-23279245, 23253475; 43596065
E-mail: discoverybooksindia@gmail.com
discoverypublishinghouse@gmail.com
web: www.discoverypublishinggroup.com

Printed at:
Infinity Imaging Systems
Delhi

Preface

The *DPH Education Handbook* has been created to provide access to information about contemporary topics in education. Practitioners and students at all levels in education have a need to know what is happening today, in addition to historical treatments within the literature.

Each chapter within the Handbook is designed to provide the user with needed "state-of-the-art" information as well as further sources of information. One of the significant features of each chapter is the inclusion of specific programmes, projects and activities so that the researcher can locate human resources as well as the literature.

The handbook will be of use to graduate and post graduate students in education and to practicing teachers, administrators, librarians and planners. The chapters and the further sources of information cited in each book should lead the reader to thousands of people and documents for either research or programme planning purposes.

An effort to achieve universal and effectiv education is based on a recognition of the rights o students to basic education that enables them t thrive in a complex society, as well as a realizatio the technological and economic growth is facilitate by increasing the numbers of students, even those with poor academic progresses, who are, in fact successful in learning. Thus, recent and current efforts improve education serve both private and social interests.

This series is addressed to administrators, planners and educators working in the field of education and training with a view to stimulating interest and attention in the areas of education and its related fields. It is also addressed to a growing number of teachers and instructors who will be practitioners in education and who will need to be acquainted with the modern aspects of educational practice and development. Many ideas, generalisations and discussions presented in this series should also prove useful to employing organisations committed to provide training facilities within their establishments—leading to effective mutual participation by institutions and organisations.

The editors wishes to thank the contributors, as well as those organizations that gave permission to publish their extracts, chapters etc.

Editors

Contents

1 Technical Education

Recent background

There are many reasons for the development of technical education during the past fifteen years. First, because the last war effort was retarded due to earlier neglect of technical education, crash programme of intensive technical education and training was instituted; but after the war complacency returned. Faith rested on the knowledge that Britain had led the world in industrialization for a hundred years.

When it became obvious by the mid-fifties that Britain was falling behind in the competition for worlds markets, immediate and long term action was required. This second reason for expanding technical education was enunciated by Sir Anthony Eden when he was Prime Minister.

'The prizes will not go to the countries with the largest populations. Those with the best system of education will win. Science and technical skill give a dozen men the power to do as much as thousands did fifty years ago. Our scientists are doing brilliant work. But if we are to make full use of what we are learning we shall need many more scientists, engineers and technicians. The aims are to strengthen the foundations of our economy to improve the standards of living of out people and to discharge effectively our manifold responsibilities overseas... One industry after another is being compelled to follow its cimpetitor, supplier or customer, in modernizing its techniques knowing that unless new materials are discovered and new methods applied British industry may fall behind in the race. The peace of change is quickening and with it the need and the demand for technical education.'

The speech preceded the 1956 White Paper *Technical Education*, which is probably the most important document ever to have appeared on technical education.

In order to produce the wealth which is needed to provided the needs and meet the obligations of an industrial nation, technical education had to be expanded. Past experience has proved that effective technical education depends on a sound foundation of primary and secondary education in mathematics, science, English, and in the development of creative imagination. It is for this reason that those responsible for technical education and industrial training want the school leaving age raised to 16 immediately, and to 18 in the foreseeable future. More parents are recognizing the career value of longer education. The number of sixth forms continues to increase. Firms are being persuaded, and are likely in the immediate future to be offered financial incentives, to train more apprentices. They are being urged to absorb larger numbers of school leavers without any fear that the nation will have an excess of skilled manpower.

Increasing productivity requires a more than proportional increase of technologists, technicians and craftsmen. Efficient British firms compare more than favourable in all respects with their foreign competitors. They have been quick to move forward with new ideas, to finance research, to modernize their equipment and organization to train the technologists and technicians. They insist on apprentices attending technical college courses to obtain the appropriate qualifications. They have efficiently staffed and equipped training workshops and schools. If factory training is not possible outside the production shops their apprentices attend apprenticeship courses centred on the local technical college.

At the opening of Churchill college in Cambirdge, Sir Winston Churchill was specific about the urgent needs and aims of scientific and technological education. 'More than any other country in the world Britain had to rely on the enterprise and trained ingenuity of her people. Since we had neither the massive populations nor the raw material, not yet adequate agricultural land to enable us to make out way in-the world with ease, we had to depend for survival on out brains- on skilled minds that were at least proportionately equal to those in the United States and Russia. The quantitative target is far from being achieved. Let none believe that the lunar rockets are merely ingenuous bids for prestige. They are the manifestations of a formidable advance in technology. As with many vehicles of pure research their immediate uses might not be apparent. But I do not doubt that they will ultimately reap a rich harvest for those who have the imagination and power to develop them and to probe ever more deeply into the mysteries of the universe in which we live.'

The chief purpose of technical education is to enable industry to meet the challenge from competing countries. Technical teachers, therefore, have a number of aims by which to direct their teaching effort:

1. To support industry and business and as a consequence the national economy.
2. To help their students to become fully effective in the practice of their careers.
3. To continue their personal, scientific, technical and general education as well as their knowledge of modern industry and business in order to e intellectually adequate to present their material in a realistic and interesting way.
4. To encourage clear thinking and flexible attitudes in their students to changing ideas in industrial organization and techniques.
5. To educate students to use their technological knowledge and skills for the common good.
6. To encourage a worthwhile use of leisure by helping students to widen their horizons.

The Four Tier System of colleges

It may be useful to recall descriptions of some of the terms which are used in discussing technical colleges and courses.

A *technologist* has the scientific and education background, the qualifications and the responsible industrial experience for membership of a professional institution. He can be a university graduate or he may have qualified at one of the technical colleges which at present produce two-thirds of the country's technologists. He has been referred to as the 'commissioned officer in the industrial army'. He functions at the higher levels of management and administration, applied research and development, design, production, planning and organization. It has been estimated to take ten years to produce a professional technologist.

A *technician* requires scientific and technical knowledge not far below that of the technologist, together with the sill of the craftsman. He is a specialist in a particular branch of an industry. He is likely to be employed as an assistant designer senior draughtsman, stressman, specialist tester or inspector, supervisor of plant installation, maintenance specialist, junior manager or foreman on the shop floor or on a building site. He may be working under the direct guidance of a technologist or he may be working alone with sole responsibility for the operation of specialist equipment. His is a comparatively new function which has to be defined from industry to industry, so that special courses can be designed for his needs. He requires a good knowledge of mathematics and science which he can apply to industrial requirements. In some industries he may be doing almost the same work as university graduates and in others it may be little more than that of a craftsman. It is estimated that about five technicians are required for every technologist in industry.

A *craftsman* is a skilled worker who has normally completed an apprenticeship. Craftsmen represent over one-third of industry' manpower. The estimated demand is for ten craftsmen to every technologists in industry. As industry becomes more complex it is becoming necessary for craftsmen to learn why they use certain tools and machines, material and techniques in particular ways for different jobs.

An *operative* is a skilled worker who does specific operations on equipment such as lathes and machine tools, or who controls special equipment such as the builders' tower crane or who carries out skilled operations in a foundry, in a textile mill, in a steel or chemical factory. Although operatives do not serve a recognized apprenticeship they usually have special training varying from a few weeks to as many years as a craftsman.

The four tier pattern of technical colleges consists of a top tier of ten colleges of advanced technology, then thirty-two regional colleges of technology, followed by an unspecified but considerable number of area technical colleges, and finally a large number of local colleges. In addition there are a very few national colleges each serving the needs of one particular industry.

Colleges of advanced technology

There are ten such colleges which were designated in the five -year period after the publication of the 1956 White Paper, *Technical Education*. They are independent of local authority control and are financed direct from the Ministry of Education. Each college has an independent governing body representative of industry, business, education and the college teaching staff. The teaching staff is highly qualified academically and is well experienced in top-level industrial management and usually has considerable research achievement. The colleges are developing post-graduate studies and higher level research. They cater for University of London external degree courses and for the qualifications of professional bodies, but the main education is for the Diploma in Technology.

At present according to official statistics 71 per cent of the courses for the Diploma in Technology are in Engineering and the remainder in applied science. A Diploma in Technology for business studies is to be introduced as a qualification towards a career in management. The Diploma in Technology is a four-year course, admission to which requires two or more General Certificate of Education passes at Advanced Level or an Ordinary National Certificate at a prescribed standard. About one quarter of the admissions are by the Ordinary National Certificate route. The courses are organized on a sandwich basis which usually means six months of the year in college and six months in industry. Students can be industry or college-based. If industry-based they are paid a salary by the firm, which also accepts responsibility for industrial training. If college-based, maintenance grants are paid through local education authorities as for University students, and the college organizes the students' industrial training. Official statistics state that 80 per cent of all engineering and 56 percent of all applied science students for the Diploma in Technology are works-based. The standard of the Diploma is equivalent to a university honours degree.

The second main course at advanced colleges leads to the Higher National Diploma in technological or business studies and to professional qualifications of a similar level. Admission requirements are about the same as for the Diploma in Technology, but the course is for those who would be unlikely to attain honours degree standard. The Higher National Diploma is considered to equate with a university pass degree. Study is on a full-time sandwich basis and students are based either in industry or college. These courses are considered to be appropriate to the regional and area colleges of technology which are the second and third tiers in the pattern.

Regional Colleges of Technology

Within the past six years thirty-two regional colleges have been designated. They do not receive a direct grant from the Ministry of Education. They are under local education authority control. The constitution of the governing bodies varies, but normally there is a considerable industrial and commercial element with representatives from neighbouring education authorities. In very few cases is there any significant teaching staff representation. The qualifications of some, but not all, of the teaching staff compare with those of colleges of advanced technology. Both kinds of college are expanding their premises, but at present only the colleges of advanced technology are building residential accommodation on a substantial scale. The regional colleges provide some courses for the Diploma in Technology but only when these are specifically required, and where they are not in competition with a college of advanced technology.

Ministry statistics show that in 1961 4,969 students enrolled in 101 Diploma in Technology courses distributed over 26 colleges; for the 1962 session the number of enrollments was 6,201 in 108 courses at 28 colleges. The immediate aim is to have 15,000 college places as soon as possible for professional technologists, increasing to 27,000 in 5 to 10 years and to over 30,000 within 12 to 15 years. Some of the development is likely to be in the regional colleges which concentrate on work beyond Ordinary National Certificate, or its equivalent the General Certificate of Education, at Advanced level.

Regional colleges also provide a large proportion of the courses for the Ordinary and Higher National Diploma and for the Ordinary and Higher National Certificate. The difference between National Diploma and National Certificate courses is that the former require full-time study usually on a sandwich basis while the latter are part-time on a block or day-release basis. Day-release means that the student is released, at present as a privilege, by his employer for one full day a week to attend the college. In addition, attendance is normally required on two evenings per week. In many cases employers cease to grant day release after the age of 18, just when most students are about to take examinations for the Ordinary National Certificate or its equivalent in craft studies. The student has then to continue to the Higher National Certificate standard usually by attendance at college on three evenings a week. Not all employers grand day-release up to the age of 18 and only a few grant it beyond the age of 21.

Block-release from industry is a comparatively new experiment by which students attend college full-time for periods varying from two weeks to three or four months at a time. The most popular arrangement is for full-time attendance for a term of twelve weeks. A sandwich course requires over eighteen weeks' continuous full-time attendance at a college and anything less, which is full-time, is labelled block-release are that the continuity and intensity of study is more effective and that the teachers and students get to know one another better. There is more time for get to know one another better. There is more time for integrating English and liberal studies with technical studies, and there are more opportunities, for developing interests in art, music, drama, handicrafts, sport and corporate activities.

Firms which support block-release find it possible to make more effective use of training facilities because they can be used every day all the year round. It allows for a larger intake of apprentices which is an important factor when trained manpower will be increasingly required in the years ahead. The educational arguments against block-release are not strong. It is said there could be such a lapse of time between blocks of attendance at college that the normal rate of forgetting would have taken its full toll. Students could lose the benefit of the continuous urge to effort provided by regular, day-a-week attendance. Most of the weaknesses are being met in a variety of ways. For example, students are required to attend on one or two evenings a week, or to continue day release between each period of block-release. The additional time is devoted to tutorial work in which the reaching effort is concentrated on helping individuals rather than in class teaching. Perhaps a more serious observation about block-release is the possibility that theory and training could get out of gear, and the pauses result in some loss of skill and retardation of practical training. A more general and controversial question is whether technical colleges should remain in session of forty-eight weeks a year in order to make the most efficient use of accommodation, equipment and industrial training facilities.

Although admission qualification to full-time National Diploma and part-time National Certificate courses are similar, the former is much broader in conception and treatment. This is likely to be reflected in two significant ways. Formerly, it was possible, for example, for an engineer having a Higher National Certificate to qualify in a fairly straight-forward way for professional technologists status as an associate member of one of the professional engineering institutions-in fact the large proportion of associate members qualified in such a way. The route is still open but it is being made so much longer and harder that in the near future it will only be possible to qualify for membership of a professional institution via a university degree, a Diploma in Technology or a Higher National Diploma. The Higher National Certificate is being increasingly regarded as the qualification of top level technicians.

One qualification for admission to a National Certificate course is four passes in specific subjects at the Ordinary level of the General Certificate of Education. It is also the qualification required for direct admission to most of the new courses being designed for higher level technicians. One of the reasons why parents want their children to remain at school until they obtain Ordinary level passes is in order to qualify for a technician apprenticeship or its commercial equivalent. It is also a reasons for encouraging General Certificate courses in secondary modern schools. The second admission qualification to National and Technician courses is by a new kind of course, the General Course. It is of either one or two years' duration and it will usually be taken straight after leaving school at a local college or its equivalent, a branch college of further education.

The regional colleges may have considerable numbers of craft students working for initial qualifications, but the aim and tendency is to shed such work, so that in future only craft students studying beyond an initial craft qualification for a technician qualification are likely to attend regional colleges. At present, however, some of the regional colleges are catering for all levels of work in technical, commercial catering and women's subjects from the Diploma in Technology at one extreme to pre-apprenticeship courses and General Courses at the other.

It is difficult at this stage of development to distinguish major differences between area and regional colleges. In the future there will probably be no degree or post-graduate studies and little technical research work being done by the staff at area colleges. A few area colleges still retain Diploma in Technology and Higher National Diploma course. Regional Councils for Further Education, which are co-ordinating bodies, decide in which colleges higher level courses are to be held in order to make the best use of regional resources. The Regional Councils endeavour to ensure that such courses will survive into the foreseeable future. They try to avoid unnecessary duplication and to concentrate advanced studies mainly in colleges of advanced technology and to lesser extent in regional colleges of technology.

Area colleges are likely to continue to have a range of Ordinary and Higher National Certificate and top-level technician courses in the technologies as well as in commercial and business studies. It may be, that, in the near future regional colleges will delegate all work below the Higher National level to area colleges. An increasing proportion of the courses in area colleges is likely to be on a block-release basis particularly in the newer kinds of courses for agriculture, catering, hotel and other seasonal occupations where adequate practical training is only possible during certain times of the year. Block-release courses are likely to be normal practice for industries in which the trained manpower exists only in small unites dispersed over wide areas. In addition to the advantages already discussed for block-release, it is also claimed that there is less student wastage than in day-release courses. Where experiments have taken place it would appear that more students complete courses successfully, in some cases obtaining two examination qualifications where previously by day-release few would have attained one qualification. The argument would be relevant for students in seasonal occupations, who may not be able to attend regularly on the same day and same two evenings every week and who, in any case, could be more subject to fatigue and more prine to monor illnesses by being over exerted during their busy seasons. The student from a small specialized firm may have to travelling distances for his day-release and two evenings' study. In such respects daily travelling to block-release would not necessarily be less unsatisfactory; hence the need for technical colleges serving areas beyond the immediate locality to have hostels or approved lodgings.

In the past, many craft students did not proceed beyond the Intermediate stage of a City and Guilds of London craft course. It is a good qualification for the majority of craftsmen but the title is considered to be unsatisfactory and is being changed to Craft Certificate. The previous higher qualification of final City and Guilds is being replaced by the Advanced Craft CErtificate which is regarded as the qualification for a top-level craftsman. To become a technician it will be necessary for a craftsman to obtain a higher qualification still, similar to the present full Technological Certificate of the City and Guilds. The courses for advanced craftsmen and for craftsmen wishing to qualify as technicians are likely to be in area colleges. The range of courses in commercial, business and women's subjects in the area colleges is as comprehensive and covers the same wide field as in regional colleges.

Local Colleges

Local colleges are suited to the further education needs of a small town catering for the majority of students up to the age of 18 or 19, by which time they will normally be expected to have reached the level of qualification required for attendance at an area or regional college. In larger towns and cities branch colleges are being established to deal with the same range of studies as local colleges in smaller towns. The technical courses as well as for secretarial and domestic subjects. Because the local college is, for most students, the first stage of further education, it is probably the most important tier in the four- tier system. The educational aim is that pupils should go straight from schools into further education. At present too many students have a year's interval after leaving school without any incentive either form parents or employers to attend a technical college. Among those who obtain apprenticeships at 16, many are not required by employers to attend college and as a result do not continue further study. Fewer still of those going into jobs not requiring apprenticeship attend a college. Until the school-leaving age is raised to 16 it is hoped that more parents will persuade their children to remain in full-time education for an additional year. If suitable courses are not available in the schools the pupils can attend the local college courses leading to Ordinary and, if they wish, to Advanced level General Certificate of Education. Statistics show that courses in colleges are catering for increasing numbers of students. Pupils remaining longer in school pursuing full-time General Certificate, pre-apprenticeship and secretarial studies in local colleges are mainly from the professional and upper-level occupational groups. 'Mostly, from smaller families and, except for secretarial courses, enrollments show a great preponderance of boys, but this is a social problem requiring a political rather than educational solution.

Another development is for industry to send its younger employees to the local college for a period of induction to further education extending from two or three weeks to as many moths. The scheme, as with all educational release by industry, is entirely dependent on the attitude of employers, so that employers with economic vision are likely to adopt it while the others ignore it. The broad aims of the induction course are to provide opportunities for educational and vocational guidance based on the techniques of diagnostic and prognostic testing; to experiment with methods of remedial and intensive teaching, particularly in mathematics and science; to work out devices for helping young people to understand the need of further vocational and general studies.

Industry is not enthusiastic about induction courses, but where pilot courses are being tried much is being learned by the staffs of local firms and local colleges. Industry as a whole is more enthusiastic about the recently introduced General Courses which are planned as an immediate educational follow-on from school, in order to maintain continuity of learning based on vocational interest. The General Courses are planned to take two years for pupils who leave school at 15, and one year for those leaving at 16 and not possessing four appropriate passes at Ordinary level of the General Certificate of Education. At present the courses are part-time day or block-release but there is increasing support for the idea that they should be on sandwich basis. They are intended to replace any existing preliminary evening courses, because it is considered that evening study by itself is an unsatisfactory and wasteful way in which to introduce school leavers to intensive technical studies.

The General Course is designed as a period during which appraisals can be made about the kinds of special vocational education courses which students should follow. The studies concentrate on mathematics and science because there is evidence that successful study in mathematics and, to lesser degree, in science is likely to lead to success in National Certificate and higher technicians' courses. There are additional subjects including drawing and English studies. As in all technical college studies, the educational aim is to encourage intellectual versatility and the rational understanding of vocationally- relevant fundamental principles, rather than to provide industrial training in precise skills and technician's course, or he may continue into th3 second year of the general course if he shows the ability for a National Certificate course. At the end of the second year he may be transferred for example to the first year of a two-year Ordinary National Certificate or Diploma course, provided he has obtained engineering drawing in the externally set and marked examination. If he has passes in these three subjects he can be transferred to the second year of the technicians' course. The student who left school at 16 and is pursuing a General Course can at the end of one year be transferred on the same basis to the first year of a National Certificate or the second year of a technician's course. All students who have completed the General Course continue attendance at the local college for two further years to obtain the Ordinary National Certificate, or for four or five years for the Advanced Craft Certificate or for a technician qualification. When the admission qualifications to National Certificate courses were accepted as either four Ordinary Level passes in specific subjects or passes with appropriate credits in the General Course, the duration of the Ordinary National Certificate courses became two years instead of three. Experience has already shown that a two-year course based on adequate admission qualifications produced a greater success rate than a three-year course without such admission qualifications. Block-release and sandwich type courses raise the success rate still further. Specialization is delayed beyond the Ordinary National stage which is usually at the age of 18 and is began at the Higher National Certificate stage. The aim is that higher technicians should have a sound understanding of fundamental principles which they can learn to apply in the automated workshops and offices designed for increased productivity. Delayed specialization allows for greater career flexibility and for adaptability within a changing pattern of industry.

Only a few Advanced Craft Certificate Courses have been introduced but as courses are being reviewed the new arrangement is being adopted. A craft student can transfer after the craft certificate stage to th first year of the National Certificate course, provided he reaches the required standard in the craft certificate examination. Specialist technician courses are being developed in association with th requirements of particular industries. Already there are courses for aeronautical engineering, metallurgical work, instrument maintenance and plastics technology. Technician courses based on further study, after final City and Guilds or Advanced Craft Certificate, are being planned for the building and furniture industries, for motor vehicle work and for printing technicians. They are known as 'end on' courses. Gradually specialist technician courses will be required and available for all industries.

It is in the local colleges that new type courses for operatives are being developed. They vary in length and they are being worked out industry by industry. They ar mainly on a day-release basis because it is accepted that no student on any course should have to depend entirely on evening study. Operatives' courses have long existed in the textile, iron, steel, chemical, boot and shoe and the coal-processing industries. Special industrial safety courses for operatives are being developed at local colleges, for example in radiation safety practice, in order to reduce the accident rate of juveniles in industry.

As an indication of the contribution by local college to industry, Ministry statistics show that 210 full-time pre-apprenticeship courses were arranged in 1961 by 82 local colleges for 4,000 school leavers. Over 3,200 apprentices, employed mostly in engineering, and some in mining and building, attended a total of 121 first year full-time industrial training and education courses arranged at 55 local and branch colleges. Each local college has a wide variety of secretarial and domestic courses. Many of the local and branch colleges have as many students studying for General Certificate examinations at Ordinary and Advanced levels as are doing so in large-sized secondary grammar schools. The growth is being encouraged because full-time education to the age of 16 is regarded as the best preparation for technical studies.

There has been tremendous emphasis in recent years on the need for closer co-operation between school, further education institutions and industry. Although philosophers have always propounded that education is for living, the tendency in the practice of the traditional education has been to ignore that living includes earning a living, and that education must include learning to earn a living. There is perpetual argument about 'living the good life' in an abstract way which ignores or is insensitive to the fact that to lice the good life requires the economic resources to support all aspects of the good life.

School and College

primary school-teachers tend to be out of touch with the social and occupational influences affecting the patterns of living of their pupils as children, as adolescents and as parents and workers. Secondary school-teachers do not seem, on the whole, to be actively concerned tha they are in large measure conditioning the technical education and career opportunities of their pupils. Although 34 per cent of boys and 7 per cent of girls leaving school go into apprenticeship and the great majority of the remainder into semi-skilled jobs, it is rarely that their teachers spend any length of time within the industries in which their pupils will spend much of their lives.

It is equally rare for school-teachers to spend time in technical colleges. Some of them want to know about Diplomas in Technology, National Course, craft qualifications, General and Induction courses, but they want to be told or to read about them. Because the pattern of technical education is larger than school education, but not by any means more complicated, school-teachers rarely make the effort to understand it. In order to excuse this attitude they infer that technical education is a mystery. The only way to learn about technical education, its aims, courses, qualifications and organization, is to become actively involved. The Ministry of Education has made many recommendations, but without much success, regarding integration of schools, further education and industry. They include: a greater and training for student teachers in university departments of education and training colleges; periods of industrial experience for all student teachers; fairly long exchanges between the staffs of schools and technical college teachers and their colleagues in industry. The individual class teacher has little control over the present situation which perpetuates educational isolation. The initiative, better quality planning and detailed arrangement is required not from individual teachers but from organizes, advisers, inspectors and the large increasing body of administrative staffs who appear, in many cases, to be concerned with anything except educational thinking and teacher guidance.

It is unfortunately true that few technical college teachers make or take opportunities for learning about secondary education. It is difficult to understand why this should be. Most Principals, Heads of Departments and Headmasters have occasional meetings and maintain a kind of superficial, educational and social contact, but technical teachers rarely spend any long period with their colleagues in the schools. It is equally difficult to understand how technical teaching can begin to be effective unless technical teachers are fully aware of the aims, content, curriculum, organization and methods of the immediately previous stage in students' education. School education is now linked very closely to technical education by the four tier system of colleges and the new kinds of vocational education courses.

The best results from further education require more effective liaison to be created between colleges and schools. Technical teachers need to learn how to use and interpret pupils' schools record cards and reports, scores in tests of attainment, ability, aptitude and personal qualities and how to correlate results with further educational and vocational guidance. They need training in the use of diagnostic tests, remedial techniques, intensive teaching methods, tutorial methods and methods based on active individual and group learning. They will need time to go into schools to make a trained study of schemes of work and teaching methods, and in particular of vocational courses including the business and industrial skill and craft subjects. In order that they may continue 'education for life and living' technical teachers must have opportunities to learn about the experimental work being done in schools in all fields of education, but particularly in the 'creative' subjects, because the country requires people with developed creative ability in order to regain a significant place in the field of industrial design, and to maintain a good standard of national culture. It is doubtful if technical education can function effectively unless it is made easy for all technical teachers to take advantage of opportunities for professional training in one form or another. Teachers without training on whole place too much reliance on methods of teaching and learning which have long been proved inadequate by any criteria.

2 The Learning Process

There are two broad types of learning which concern the technical teacher. One is unwitting learning which requires no conscious effort from the student; the second is deliberate learning, which does.

Unwitting learning

In this type of learning the teacher's personal example and the learning environment he creates are more important than teaching methods or technique. It is from living with teachers who have attitudes of understanding and social responsibility what students are likely to build desirable qualities of character and personality. The teacher's manner, speech, level of personal culture and thinking all influence the students' outlook. His enthusiasm for his subject and its industrial applications as well as his attitudes to work and study are examples to th students.

Deliberate learning

This type depends on th student having an adequate motive for making the effort to learn. The organization of motives to stimulate and sustain interest and effort depends largely on the teacher's knowledge of the relationship between technical education, industry and society. Probably the strongest learning motive is the student's desire to become more proficient at his job. He is willing to study if he is convinced that as a result he will be a better technician, craftsman, secretary or business worker. Failure by the teacher to be convincing about the vocational relevance of his lessons results in lack of interest and willingness to learn. To capitalize on the career motive the teacher has to be abreast of the applications of technology to modern industry. It is a common criticism of technical teachers that their lessons are too elementary, too theoretical, and too remote from the working experience of students.

Passing examinations is an important learning motive. Students know that by passing the appropriate examinations they can attain qualifications leading to better, more highly paid, more secure jobs at higher occupational levels giving enhanced social prestige. Students enrol for courses with the aim of passing examinations and they have every right to expect success. The simple motive of learning to do a good job for its won sake appeals to only the few students who may not want promotion, or who realize they are not suited for it. Whatever motives are used, promotion, job satisfaction or better citizenship, the teacher has to make them obvious and convincing to the students.

The three kinds of deliberate learning which concern the technical teacher are Rote, Rule-of-Thumb and Rational.

Rote Learning

Acquiring workshop, office or laboratory techniques depends largely on the rote learning of relevant skills by their incorporation in repetitions of similar operations dependent on the application of the skills and good working habits. From the technical teacher's point of view the problem is that repetition gives rise to boredom and fatigue are not know, a considerable body on information is available about it. It does not affect all students simultaneously, or in similar ways. It is difficult to anticipate and not easy to avid. The symptoms include gradual loss of concentration and interest, restlessness, irritability, an increase in careless mistakes, and minor accidents. There are ways of delaying its effects. A draught free flow of fresh air and a comfortable temperature, both depending on the nature and intensity of student activity help to postpone the onset of fatigue.

Work-study planning, including job and time analysis, can provide immediately foreseeable, attainable targets of achievement. Student performance in relation to achievement targets provides a device for 'progressing' the students at short intervals. Personal responsibility and enthusiasm for learning are fostered when students are informed regularly of their progress. Attainable goals help to advance learning when they are planned in relation to each student's level of general ability. They want to know is they are doing better, worse, or just the same as last week, if they are likely to obtain a good pass, a near pass or to fail the examination. They want to know if they are achieving the appropriate targets. Records of progress are therefore an essential aid to skill learning. The student is given the incentive to improve on his won performance. The job, or skill exercise, analysis allows for assessments on a five-point scale, A to E, which can be combined to give a final assessment. Because the student's practical work is progressed section by section during each learning period mistakes are not perpetuated throughout practices. For the same reason it is better to check mathematical examples as each one is completed, rather than delay checking until several problems involving a specific process have been completed. Equally, it is unfair to allow students to devote hours to chemical analysis and calculation doomed to repetition, because of an error in technique or application which could have been rectified at an early point in a progressed procedure. Hurried or careless planning and lack of individual progressing by the teacher can produce unnecessary boredom and fatigue, with the accompanying frustrations causing resentment to learning and revulsion from the subjects involved.

Motion study can be applied to planning the least fatiguing layout for the use of tools, equipment and workroom fittings.

Adequate lighting, fitted and placed for maximum illumination without glare or dangerous reflection, delays the onset of fatigue. When it becomes apparent by the decline in learning interest that fatigue can no longer be delayed the teacher has to change the activity. This does not necessarily involve a complete break. The change can be an informal discussion. For example, the teacher of workshop practice can introduce an exchange of ideas about how a working drawing is initiated, built up, processed and used when planning a job, or discuss the historical development of the tools, machines, materials being used, or the techniques of their manufacture and maintenance. The short breaks are useful times for discussing safety precautions, storekeeping procedure, or the principle of workshop planning and organization. Discussion could extend to the more liberal aspects of craft history, the pioneers of new methods and materials or the growth of craft institutions.

Teaching methods for subjects dependent on repetitive learning can be devised by the technical teacher from an analysis of errors made by students. The analysis of learners' errors is a normal basis for devising teaching methods in primary and secondary schools. It has been applied to reading, mathematics, science and English.

It is also possible to plan training exercises 'off the job' to develop some of the muscular co-ordination necessary for practical skills. On the continent the technique has been specially adapted to learning such fine skills as garment cutting and tailoring, and at the other extreme for the physical training of youths preparing for heavy work in electrical power transmission. Apart from creating interest which delays boredom and fatigue, the planning and co-ordination of theoretical subjects around their practical applications is recognized as one of the most effective approaches to students attending technical courses.

Rule-of-Thumb learning

This means learning without gaining insight or understanding. It has restricted value in technical teaching. It should be confined to those subjects to which the students, because of their educational equipment, cannot understand the scientific and mathematical background. It is at its poorest when students are required to regurgitate statements of scientific laws without understanding how the laws have originated or how they are applied in technology. Word-perfect recitations of the laws of moments, for example, are intellectual lumber to an apprentice who strips a screw thread because he has used the wrong kind of spanner. Ability to recite the principles of bonding is useless to a brick-layer unable to make a scientific choice of the best kind of bonding for a particular job. Tailoring students are using rule-of-thumb, mechanical, learning in pattern-drafting when following an exact numbered sequence from one fixed point suitable points, or why they were chosen in the first place. Learning mathematical formulae without understanding is unnecessary when most of those required by technical students can be illustrated and applied by using visual aids. It is the kind of learning which destroys the interest of apprentices whose minds are nimble and curious about the how and why of the principles of their vocation.

Rational learning

This is the best kind of learning for technical students because it means learning by activity following the connected chain of thought in the logical development of a subject. It depends on the teacher analysing and presenting material as a progressively reasoned argument. For example, in teaching the principles and use of the spray-gun to apprentice painters the line of reasoning could be:

1. Eliciting, by question and answer, from the class the requirements of the spray-gun in relation to the jobs it has to do.

2. Teaching the scientific principles by which each requirement is met and by which the spray-gun operates.

3. Illustrating and demonstrating the assembly details of the spray-gun in relation to the principles of operation.

4. Demonstration of the method of using the spray-gun to show how the principles of operation and assemble apply in practice.

5. Discussion on the care and maintenance of the spraygun.

For teaching a scientific law or principle the analysis and line or reasoning might be:

1. Observation by the students of experiments to show a number of examples of the law or principle.

2. The students make compressions from the data obtained from observations.

3. The students make their own deductions from the comparison of data.

4. A statement, in words and symbols, of the scientific relationships perceived.

5. Tests of the reliability of these relationships

6. Application of the law or principle by the students to actual industrial situations.

An example of rational learning applied to the properties of a material might be:

1. Small groups of students carry out the various tests on steels of different carbon content.

2. Data collected to calculate different properties in relation to different loads.

3. Graphs drawn.

4. Required information extracted from the graph concerning relationship between stress and strain for each test specimen, elastic limit, yield point, ultimate stress, breasing point.

5. Comparisons made for variations in carbon content.

6. Judgments made about the uses of steels of different carbon content for different purposes.

The tests could be extended, as required by the syllabus, to include compression, shearing, hardness, malleability., fatigue, tension, toughness and for different heat treatments, alloying contents and the effects of different working conditions. Comparisons and deductions could be made about how and why particular proprieties vary, and judgments formed about the particular grade of material suitable for a job subject to prescribed physical and chemical working conditions.

A learning analysis for the production of a material might be:

1. The natural sources of the raw material elicited by question and answer.

2. The impurities in the raw metrical at its source elicited from the students.

3 Demonstrations and teaching aids used to show that industrial production of the material means applying scientific principles such as flotation, filtering, oxidation, reduction, crystallization, distillation, electrolysis.

4. Flow diagrams drawn to show what happens at each stage of production.
5. The proprieties and uses presented as suggested in the previous example.

The technique or writing simple technical reports can also be learned rationally by the analysis of actual examples from local industry. The aim in teaching report writing is that students should learn to produce fully informative documents which are concise and unambiguous. The teaching might be planned in this way:

1. Visits to local firms by the teachers to collect appropriate examples and to make an analysis of the kind of information appearing in actual reports. Too many teachers of English subjects in technical colleges remain unfamiliar with the industrial duties of technicians and higher level craftsmen who are frequently required to prepare reports for the management. Many teachers of English ignore the industrial applications of English and concentrate on perpetuating English composition, precis writing, comprehension, remedial exercises in grammar and spelling.
2. Discussions with industrial staffs to gather ideas and views on how to compile and present technical reports. This kind of information cannot be gleaned from text books.
3. From the information supplied by industry, students select, discuss, analyse and rearrange relevant material for presentation in a logical way to a works manager.

4. The exercise is attempted by each student.
5. The exercises are corrected and discussed in a constructive way, from which students learn how and why modifications have to be made.
6. The individual efforts are improved by repetition.
7. Final comparisons are made with an actual report on the same subject.

Because it is sometimes difficult, and always time consuming, to organize a technical topic so that students can pursue a chain of connected thought from lesson to lesson, many technical teachers still continue to 'tell' students by giving formal lectures. They persist in teaching as they were taught. They probably find it difficult and unattractive to learn and to practice more rational methods. But technical qualifications, and teaching or industrial experience, are without value until they are critically appraised and organized for rational learning.

Aids to Learning

A strong personal motive is the best aid to learning. Materialistic individual gain, self-advancement and self-enhancement motives are unfortunately the most effective. Ideally, more altruistic motives should be at least as effective. In fairness to youth and to students it has to be said that no section of society has yet found an answer to educating people in the obligation of putting full personal energy into the communal effort. In industry and business, and as a consequence in technical education, personal promotion and personal power incentives and values appear to be more significant than altruistic motives. They are less obviously emphasized, but equally present in the more traditional and academic occupations. The technical teacher has a difficult task in deciding how far he should emphasize personal motives at the risk of neglecting social and liberal education.

Co-ordinating the different subjects in a technical course to form one complete body of knowledge is an important aid to learning. Individual subjects tend to be taught by specialist teachers functioning in isolation. As a result students regard their studies as a number of unconnected specializations. Subjects isolation destroys the unified-course motive, so that effort varies between subjects, usually according to the teaching ability and enthusiasm of the different teachers. The British system of technical education tends to fragment courses so that each subject, however elementary, is taken by a separate teacher. For example, for one class a different teacher may be responsible for shorthand, typing, English, commerce, book-keeping, office routine, secretarial practice. At the early stages of craft courses it is common for a different teacher to be responsible in one class for calculations, craft science, technology, workshop practice, drawing, English subjects. With such an organization, course co-ordination is virtually impossible. The continental system is more satisfactory because one technical teacher takes the same class for the first three years of vocational studies in all subjects including language and civics.

Detailed interlocking of the subjects in a course depends on successful teaching experience and an understanding of the full course and its aims as well as its applicability to industry. It also depends on having first-hand knowledge of the individual differences of students. Subject co-ordination should be the most important and most time demanding function of the senior members of the technical teaching staff. Some examining bodies produce partly co-ordinated schemes of work but the ultimate task is quite specifically the responsibility of Heads of Departments if integration is to be effective. The use of the vocational motive as a learning aid by integrating college studies and industrial training is also the responsibility of senior teaching and training staffs. The class teacher does not have the knowledge, experience, time or professional status to undertake such highly skilled responsible tasks of planning and co-ordination.

Creating anticipatory interest is a good aid to learning. It can be encouraged by giving students at the beginning of each term a list of lessons with their specific aims, and an information. It provides a sense of direction and urgency, guidance and cohesion and a feeling of moving forward which is fundamental to rational learning. The complete antithesis to planning is when students are unaware of what is to be learned until a lesson is nearly finished, or when the teacher's opening gambit is a request for information about the subject matter of the previous lesson.

When workmates and immediate superiors are openly cynical about the value of college studies it has a discouraging effect on the student. not all students have the stimulus of parental encouragement. In both instances the teacher has to make a particular effort to convince the student of the value of technical studies. It is also important that whether a student has ten talents or five talents he should be using all of them. It is wrong to retard the bright student to the rate of the slow student and it is futile to attempt to accelerate all class learning to the rate of the brightest students. Teaching to the average is a myth, however, vociferously it is justified and defended.

The quality of schools education can be considerable help or hindrance to technical college study. For example, a student from a school having a high success rate and reputation in mathematics is likely to be good at the subject and keen to continue learning it. A student from a school with a good record in teaching handicrafts and associated subjects is likely to learn technical subjects better than a student from a less encouraging background. Learning practical subjects if further aided if the student comes from a home in which it is normal to use tools for hobbies and maintenance work.

Teaching new students to organize their time and their studies, how to use libraries and how to find information readily and maintain notes are valuable fundamental aids to learning.

Remembering

For the technical student remembering means more than memorizing or having information stored in his mind. It is the ability to recall what has been learned for use when required. The teacher has to bear in mind that much of what he teachers is forgotten during the lesson period, a great deal more is forgotten by the end of the day and practically everything by the end of a month. He has to ensure that learning is well established in the course of each lesson in order to reduce the rate of forgetting. One methods is to make certain by the quality of lesson presentation that interest and have understood by reasoning. Remembering is enhanced when learning appeals to all the senses. It helps if students make their own observations, comparisons, deductions, and formulate their own ideas about how and why things function. They can recall fundamental principles most easily when they have discovered them by carrying out experiments, or from demonstrations, or by using the library , or by working on projects, assignments or case studies. Remembering is greatly assisted when the teacher uses the black-broad, conducts demonstration, uses films, pictures, charts, diagrams, and models. Teaching aids nee to be an integral part of every technical lesson regardless of its subject matter. Students also remember whatever they have felt to be worthwhile and vocationally relevant during their lessons. They recall material which was connected logically to associations and other ideas already in their minds.

Recapitulation of freshly-taught subject matter with its old and new associations is a necessary aid to remembering. Students can recall easily the pleasant things and they forget most quickly those having, unpleasant, unattractive associations. Recapitulation is necessary as the lesson proceeds. Time has to be left near the end of the lesson for consolidation which can be reinforced by homework. With regular recapitulation from lesson to lesson there is little need for long periods of revision which can easily become an unreasonable encroachment on students' learning time. Concentration or revision, often with its special place on the time-table and sometimes consuming all the learning time for weeks before and examination, gives a mistaken sense of climax when the examination is over. It can be an interesting experiment for a teacher to total the time devoted to revision, testing. and examining and then to subtract it from the time devoted to teaching new subject matter. In some cases examinations, internal and external, terminal and sessional, together with preparations for them and the marking after them consume unproductively more than a third of each term. With such misuse of time it is little wonder that syllabuses are claimed misuse of times it is little wonder that syllabuses are claimed to be too overcrowed for completion in the time available.

3 Factors in Learning

Few students regard technical education as a privilege which in fact it is not, in an industrial society dependent on expanding productivity for survival. They know they must be educated and trained for highly-skilled occupations in order to maintain and raise standards of living at home and overseas. But some are disinterested in such training.

Technical teachers in a modern industrial society cannot reject the apathetic or antipathetic. It is relatively easy to teach keen students but particularly rare teaching skill is required to stimulate interest in those unwilling to learn. Because such students find concentration and the will-power for sustained thinking beyond them, it would be wrong to assume that they cannot be taught. The teacher has to combine his skills and enthusiasm to experiment with teaching methods. Some students oppose the teacher in a pleasant and intellectually stimulating way. They challenge for the joy of the cut and thrust of argument. It is only occasionally that a student is sullen and rude. If asked, he probably could not explain his attitude. The sensible teacher ignores it; he certainly does not create an incident. Students feel that some of their teachers are out of data in their thinking, have inflexible, one-track minds and only a limited knowledge of modern industrial practice. They want independence from anything reminiscent of school discipline, from he control of home and parents, from adult authority. They rebel against superior attitudes, bullying and unfairness. They are intolerant of teachers who have vegetated intellectually. They do not believe that age is synonymous with wisdom or that years of experience equate with technical knowledge. They can be unkind and intolerant of those who do not subscribe to views which confirm their own, or even of those who are weak or crippled. They can be irresponsible towards the obligations of the adulthood they demand. They express their unformed ideas crudely and dogmatically. Some can be perverse but few are vicious. The actions of the vicious are over publicized. Anti-social adolescents appear to be more interesting than normal students to the journalist, sociologist and cleric: perhaps this is as sit should be. The overwhelming majority of technical students are normal human beings behaving with as little self-seeking sensationalism as their parents, employers and teachers.

Students are willing to make the effort to learn to think systematically and accurately. They prefer to study under pressure than to conform to a leisurely routine. They prefer to be allocated worthwhile homework and to have it marked regularly and efficiently than to be left with no organized assignments to complete. They require a weekly summing up and a regular review to convince them of progress. They welcome individual discussions and tutorials with their teachers. They prefer learning based on reasoning and understanding to formal lecturing and 'telling'. They enjoy laboratory experiments and workshop exercises, solving problems and working out the facts for themselves. Their intellectual capacity is frequently underestimated by teachers using old fashioned, uninteresting, thoroughly boring rule-of-thumb teaching methods. They tend to be too energetic and to attempt too much physical activity for their strength. The teacher has to realize and make allowances in his planning for the fact that they are growing rapidly and that not all parts of their bodies develop in harmony. Some can be clumsy in co-ordinating their movements for precision work in notebooks, on the drawing-board, in the laboratory or workshop. They need encouragement rather than blame at this stage of their physical growing. Too heavy or too constant physical effort must be avoided. Full use has to be made of motion study in workshop and laboratory in order to make economic use of energy. Technical college students, like all adolescent workers, have problems of adjustments to their own kind of society. They have to come to terms with the discipline of industry and its different interpretations of loyalty, standards, codes of behaviour and values from those pertaining at school and home. They have to learn very quickly to accept responsibility for making their own decisions. They have to come to terms with being self-supporting wage-earners trying to make the best use of their money. They are subjected to the allures of teenage advertising. At work they meet and are often confused by the industrial class structre and by the emotions evoked by workds like boss, management, foreman, shop steward, union, organization and method, work-study, fair day's work and fair day's pay. They are subject to all sorts of propaganda from the political parties which they are often unable to evaluate. They have difficulty in establishing values, in recognizing and choosing between what is fundamentally right and wrong. They can be irritatingly, but rightly scornful of the academic discussions which take place on these subjects in many social studies classes in technical colleges. For students the issues are not theoretical. They are actively involved, and words have combustible overtones when interpreted by different people according to their social or industrial status. For example, the student in industry has to broaden his loyalty beyond school, college, individuals or any system. It has to be reinterpreted to include commitments within the large and complicated organism of the working community to which he belongs.

Intelligence

The ease with which a student can learn depends largely on his general mental ability. Standardized tests are used to measure the rate of mental development. If a 10-year-old is able to go as far up the standardized scale as the average 8-year-old, he will have a mental age of 8 years or 80 per cent of normal intelligence. His intelligence quotient is 80. If a child whose chronological age is 8 years has a mental age of 10 years, his rate of mental development is one and a quarter, 1.25, that of an ordinary 8-year-old. His intelligence quotient is 1125. The 'near genius' has an I.Q of 140 plus; the normal is between 80 and 110, dull is from 80 to 90 and from 0 to 25 idiot.

From the considerable literature available on the subject it seems that I.Q. is fairly steady from the age of 5 onwards. It can be influenced to some extent by coaching, or by becoming used to the tests. It is said to be influenced by both heredity and environment. But some dull parents have bright children. There is said to be a larger proportion of bright children from upper-class professional homes than from lower-class or non-professional homes, but because of the greater overall numbers the total of bright children is greater from non-professional than professional homes. I.Q. is not the same as acquired technical or academic knowledge.

In some cases there is no increase in I.Q. after the age of 13 and a slight decline may start at about 18 and fluctuates can occur until nearly 26. ITs continued development appears to be related to length of formal education, intellectual demands of employment and to the nature of leisure-time activities.

A high I.Q. is claimed to be indicative of a capacity for original thinking and maintaining directed thought, for reasoning and understanding. In the past the result of there being more bright young people than jobs available was to set standards of recruitment for some occupations far above required ability levels. Banking, insurance and the distributive trades are examples of occupations which have had to lower admission standards to a more realistic level in a world where bright school-leavers seek employment with firms having up-to-data education and training schemes and in which their talents can lead quickly to the highest posts within the organization. Even people in the low ranges of ability are able to do jobs considered beyond their reach in the past. Some of the previously unemployable because of their very low intelligence are now able, as a result of new training techniques, to be almost fully self-supporting.

The technical teacher has to ensure that the student of average I.Q. who also has interest and persistence should have every opportunity to learn. The teacher may argue that low I.Q. and backwardness go together, but he has also to accept the evidence that a normal I.Q. and poor achievement tolerate routine class discipline. They cannot bear the drudgery of mechanical learning and remembering. If they are subjected to mediocre, poorly planned, unexciting teaching they inevitably apply their ability to making life uncomfortable for the teacher. Dull students are never a nuisance. They ask only to be left alone.

Aptitude

Aptitudes are special, latent indicators of an individual's capacity and potentiality in a particular group of activities. Aptitude for a subject encourages the necessary interest for successful learning, Changes in aptitude are rare and normally within predictable limits. The pattern of his aptitudes is an important part of an individual's personality.

Tests are being devised to identify the aptitudes needed to acquire the knowledge and skills suited to particular activities. Tests are available to measure visual abilities, mechanical and assembly aptitudes, verbal fluency, manual dexterity and aptitude for drawing, artistic and musical abilities, ability in number.

Large numbers of occupations are being broken down and analysed in an attempt to isolate the aptitudes required for particular groups of jobs and to construct test to identify them. From test scores individual student profiles are constructed as a basis for guidance. The information provided by such profits needs to be supplemented by school records, examination results and information about the individual's general ability.

During the final years in school a wide curriculum of theoretical and practical activities can provide scope for children's aptitudes and inclinations to become apparent. Too early vocational specialization can permanently categorize an individual before all his potentialities are known. One of the purposes of induction and general courses in technical education is to provide educational guidance by studying students over a fairly long period. Teachers can be trained to administer tests suited to all grades of ability.

Home background

It is at home that the student establishes the standards and values by which he lives. These in turn determine persistence, willingness to work to capacity, readiness to learn and reactions to advice and guidance. His parents will have encouraged or frustrated an intelligent curiosity about the world around him, and his choice of ways to satisfy it. He will have learned to co-operate with teachers or to resist them. In short, his attitudes towards education and career advancement will have been influenced by those of his parents and their social group. It is, therefore, important for all those concerned with education to work for the removal of the adverse social factors inhibiting the full use of abilities. This is a task for government, employers, trade unions, teachers, parents, education authorities, professional bodies and society as a whole.

Industry

The greatest stimulus which any firm can give students is to release them from work to take advantage of technical education. Firms making no educational provision are not discharging their responsibility either to young employees or to the country. There are still too many firms which respond by dumb resistance to Government appeals. Even less praiseworthy are those firms requiring evening class attendance as a condition of employment without granting day release. It should be made clear to industry that college principals and technical teachers are too scarce to waste their teaching time begging interviews hoping to persuade recalcitrant employers to release their young employees for courses of technical studies. This should be work for the Government, the central executive and local administration.

Persuasion from any source has so far made little impact. The central executive has produced many first-class, objectives, far-seeing reports full of sound ideas and workable plans which, if implemented by industry as a whole, would in less than a decade achieve the publicized aim of 'doubling the standard of living, and giving every worker at least a thousand a year'. Anyhow, the decade for which that was hoped has almost gone and there is higher unemployment now than at its beginning. The burden of evening study only on young people is made no less by the naive incentives of workshops by the apprentices themselves, as prizes for regular attendance and outstanding achievement in evening studies. Firms arranging shift work so that students can attend part-time day classes, while insisting that a full working week is c completed by an additional shift, are no better than those requiring day release to be made up by working overtime. Unfortunately the same kind of thinking can be encountered in education. For example, some technical teachers cannot have release for any courses of study or training during the working week. In other cases they are released only provided they make up the time by teaching evening classes or compressing a full-time load into a shortened week. It is sad that a small proportion of the education hierarchy can be more grudging towards education and training opportunities for technical teachers than the most hostile industrial employer.

Learning is encouraged when the liaison between the firm and college is adequate. If managers and their immediate subordinates occasionally sat in at technical college lessons it would convince students that their superiors are not too busy, or too uninterested, to be concerned with the progress of young people who will be the technicians and craft force of the firm's immediate future. The practice would convince teachers that their work is properly understood by industry. It would provide a basis for informal exchange of ideas and information. Principals could arrange for groups of teachers to meet industrial members of advisory committees to discuss details of schemes of work and teaching methods. Unfortunately, many advisory committees meet only once a year, without any teaching staff present, to do little more than recommend annual estimates and to rubber stamp decisions already taken by senior staff in the college. Whatever techniques can be devised to enhance the quality of education and training integration will have a good effect.

Teachers need to visit local firms regularly, and probably at least weekly, to obtain technical advice and guidance, to learn new skills and techniques, to discuss and observe processes and operations, to learn how to make every technical lesson count by relating it in a convincing way to local industrial practices. It is useful to have penetrative, objective, uninhibited exchanges with industrial colleagues about the quality of teaching and works training, as they are related to one another. Teachers should go into firms annually for periods of not less than four full weeks at a time. Without such experience the technical teacher can only be 'talking about industry' from a hazy memory of the practices of a year or more ago. Younger technical teachers should be made aware that the Ministry of Education and most governing bodies encourage returning to industry for periods of up to a year with salary and superannuation rights maintained. Most firms welcome applications but the unfortunate fact is that very few requests are made by technical teachers. It may be that principals and heads of departments do not make the necessary arrangements, or include regular returns to industry as a normal condition of engagement, or bring sufficient evidence to bear on governing bodies to convince them that adequate staff is necessary to meet all departmental needs. It must constitute a serious reflection on any technical teacher who does not recognize and accept the need for continual close association with industry.

When a manager, an executive or a department superintendent takes a personal interest in the education of students it provides them with an incentive to learn. There is a positive influence on student morale when time is made to discuss notebook contents, progress to education and training, difficulties with studies, prospects of advancement and the broad non-vocational interests of the student.. In being critical, the discussion has to be constructive and directed towards improving the integration between college and firm. Just to function as a paternal but remote hierarchy issuing an occasional memorandum of praise or reproof can be more irritating to young people than being ignored.

Teachers

Although a knowledge of his subjects is the most important attribute of a technical teacher, he must also be interested in the whole field of education in order to get his own part in correct perspective. Understanding the principles of learning gives the teacher the necessary background for effective preparation, planning and presentation, and for keeping his methods up to date. By reflection on his own student days the teacher can be objective about some of the causes of learning difficulties.

He needs to have answers to the questions: What does technical education involve? How does it differ from vocational training? How does it differ from any other job I have ever done? Why am I teaching? Am I justifying my function?

Self-appraisal can be a useful counteraction to any tendency the teacher may have to take his work of his students' needs for granted. It can convince the teacher of the value of his contribution to an industrial society. He appreciates that a good teacher must keep his subject and industrial knowledge at a high level. He welcomes opportunities of co-operating with colleagues in college and industry to devise teaching methods encouraging all-out learning effort by the students. Self-criticism need not be confused with being self-deprecating. The teacher alone can decide if he is as physically fit and even-tempered and in control of situations as he ought to be. He has to evaluate his preparation for lesson content and method of presentation. The adequate teacher knows that students are quick to sense the insincerity of careless preparation and are impatient of slovenly presentation. It is always a problem of self-appraisal for the teacher to decide whether he or the class talked too much or too little and whether he was amusing or irritating, stimulating or dreary. In his determination to do a good job the teacher may give students the idea that he is dogmatic, and self-important. He needs to reflect on his speech and delivery; is it too loud, too slow or too fast? Has he expressed his meaning clearly? Being human, the teacher finds that some students attract him more than others and he makes allowances for bias. Old-fashioned teachers over-emphasize strict authoritarian discipline. When they are responsible for overseeing the work of younger and often more enlightened teachers, it can cause anxiety because the latter are afraid of not being sufficiently strict. Of course, they need not be concerned; severe discipline and tight control have never achieved any worthwhile aims in technical or in any other kind of education.

Much has been written on the qualities of the good teacher but there is little agreement about how he functions in practice because good teachers do not conform to a pattern.

One thing that can be said is that they all provide guidance and inspiration, each in his particular individual fashion. No doubt, there are some born teachers just as there are born doctors or engineers, but their potentiality can only be made fully effective by training, and experience.

4 Technical Education: Its Structure

There is no universally accepted definition of Technical Education. It varies from country to country and is sometimes identified by particular types of institutions and their courses of study. In India, Technical Education represents a complex of activities that include post-graduate courses and research; under-graduate course leading to a first degree or equivalent award: diploma courses; certificate courses; junior technical schools and technical studies at secondary school level; apprenticeship etc. The predominant characteristic of technical education is what may be called the "double finality" of educational development for the individual and the acquisition by him of techniques and skill. The emphasis on the one or the other may vary from course to course; the organisational arrangements may differ; or the types of institutions may be diverse. But both form essential components of technical education.

Technologist or technician?

The terms Engineering and Technology are sometimes used synonymously and sometimes differently, to distinguish between different subjects. Technical institutions are sometimes referred to as engineering colleges; sometimes as technological colleges; and in some cases as colleges of engineering and technology. There is no doubt that a certain amount of terminological confusion exists, but this is more in usage than in basic concept. Historically engineering included only the more well-known fields such as Civil Engineering, Mechanical Engineering and Electrical Engineering. As the application of science to industry widened and the forces of Nature were harnessed increasingly for the material prosperity of man, a large body of applied scientific knowledge grew up and was called by the more comprehensive term Technology. Technology, therefore. includes all fields of engineering and applied sciences that are responsible for present-day progress.

Confusion has also arisen out of the fact that between the two words, Technologist and Technician which sound and look alike there is a wide difference though the words are often used synonymously. A trained technician may be defined as a person who, without aspiring ever to reach one of the directing positions in industry, is nevertheless fully competent to understand, control and maintain the technical processes committed to his charge. A technologist, on the other hand, is a person capable of appreciating the latest progress in research laboratories and applying scientific knowledge and methods to industry.. This distinction between a technologist and a technician is important since it determines the standard and scope of technical education at different levels. The Commonwealth Education Conference formulated the following definitions:

Technologist: A person holding a degree or equivalent professional qualification in science or engineering, who is responsible for the application of scientific knowledge and method to industry.

Technician: A person qualified by specialist technical education and practical training to work under the general direction of a technologist

Craftsman: Normally, a person who has served a recognised apprentice-ship in a trade and who applies his skills on the shop floor.

The definitions explain in the best way possible the nature and scope of technical education and training at three main levels.

Four-tired structure

Technical education in India is a four-tiered structure comprising post-graduate courses and research; first degree courses; diploma courses; and vocational or industrial training. Each tier is a self-contained aspect intended to serve a specific purpose and neither the diploma courses nor the industrial training courses are a preparation for the next higher tier.

For post-graduate courses and research, however, only those candidates who have a first degree in the relevant subjects are admitted. The objective of the first degree courses is to train technologists, some of whom may eventually become designers, research engineers or specialists in various fields either after further studies at post-graduate level or experience in the profession. they are not concerned with preparing persons for specific positions or jobs in industry, but with giving them a broad-based education in the scientific principles and methods underlying technology. Equally, they are not concerned to develop particular technical skills in students but to acquaint them with various production methods in accordance with constructional requirements in a system that consists of an assembly of men, materials and machines.

First degree courses

Till recently, the duration of first degree courses was general four years with the Intermediate in Science as the minimum admission qualification. The Intermediate in Science, a preparatory stage for university courses was of two years' duration after a high school education that extended over a period generally of ten years. It therefore took six years for a student to complete the first degree after his high school education.

Secondary education in the country is in process of re-organisation and the new pattern envisages an eleven-year schooling intended to prepare candidates for life and for direct entry to university. The existing Intermediate course is being abolished. As a result of this change, the first degree course are being re-organised into a five-year integrated course after higher secondary education. The advantages of a five-year integrated course are: first, a more fruitful integration of fundamental sciences, technological subjects and liberal arts will be possible. Second, a higher level of scientific and technical competence may be expected since the students can absorb the different subjects in more suitable stages and in the right combinations. Third,

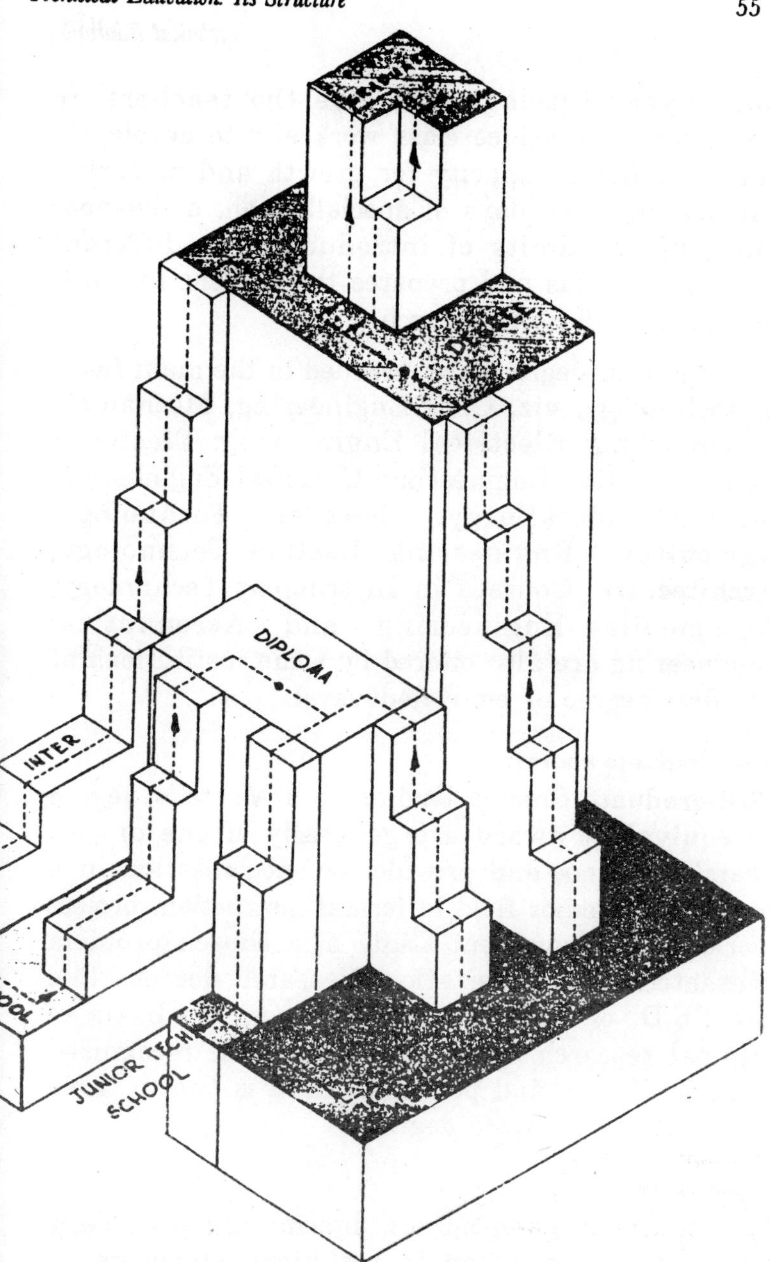

Structure of technical education

a five-year tutelage will give the teachers an opportunity to reduce class work and to develop in the students a capacity for growth and maturity. Finally, in these days of specialisation, a five-year curriculum admits of introduction to different specialised fields and prepares the student for post-graduate studies or research.

The first degrees are awarded in the main fields of technology, viz. Civil Engineering; Mechanical Engineering; Electrical Engineering; Electrical Communication Engineering; Chemical Engineering; Mining; Metallurgy; Textiles Technology; Agricultural Engineering; Leather Technology; Architecture. Courses in Instrument Technology, Automobile Engineering and Aeronautical Engineering are also offered by some institutions at the first degree or equivalent level.

Post-Graduate courses

Post-graduate courses leading to a Master's degree or equivalent award are generally of one or two years' duration, and provide for specialisation in a branch of a major field in formal instruction, project work and independent study of a chosen problem presented as a dissertation. Research degrees like the Ph.D. or D.Sc. are awarded on the basis of original research done by candidates at recognised centers. The normal period required is two to three years after a Master's degree.

Diploma courses

Next to first degree courses, diploma courses occupy an important position in technical education in India. These courses are conducted by a large number of institutions called Polytechnics and Rural

Institutes and are designed to train technicians who will eventually occupy supervisory positions like foreman, overseers etc., in industry and other technical organisations, in charge of engineering construction, production and operation and maintenance. Another function that the diploma-holders can perform is as engineer aide in design offices or on the shop floor or on field execution. The courses are three yeas long after a high school education and have a strong practical bias. The view has, however, been advanced in recent years that the practical knowledge and experience required by a technician cannot be given to him in an adequate measure in a course that in wholly institution-based, and that the present three-year diploma courses do not always produced the right type of personnel. The All India Council for technical Education has therefore designed a Sandwich Course of four years for diploma in mechanical engineering. In this course, practical training in industry and institutional studies alternate in suitable layers. The student spends stated periods in industry and in an educational institution, throughout the course and fulfills the academic requirements for the diploma. He also gains the practical experience necessary for a supervisory position. The scheme has been introduced at selected centers in co-operation with industry. The sandwich pattern is now the normal form of training technicians for mining industry, and has been adopted at all the mining schools. As training facilities in industry expand, the sandwich course will become an important feature of technical education in India.

The diploma courses are offered in the main fields of civil, mechanical and electrical engineering. A few institutions also offer Textile Technology, Leather Technology,Mining Engineering and other fields according to regional requirements for technical personnel at this level.

As a matter of established usage, the term "Polytechnic" represents in India today technical institutions that conduct diploma courses chiefly in civil, mechanical and electrical engineering. It indicates at once both the standard of training and the main fields of study. Except for a few institutions that are under the direct control of universities, all polytechnics are affiliated to State Boards of Technical Education in different States. The State Boards prescribe the courses of study, conduct examinations and award diplomas. Uniformity of standards on an All-India basis is maintained through the All-India Council for Technical Education which has formulated National Certificate course to serve as a model for the diploma courses conducted at polytechnics.

Technical training at secondary stage

The Indian Constitution makes it essential for the State to provide free compulsory education for all children up to the age of 14 i.e. up to three classes below the new higher secondary course that is in process of being introduced. The question is how to provide diversified opportunities for education and training to a majority of students after 14, for gainful occupation in life. The issue partly arises from the fact that secondary education is a terminus for a majority of students and so, has to be a self-sufficient and practical preparation for entry to life.

It is partly due also to the fact that the present menace of large numbers of students crowding aimlessly into universities and other higher institutions has to be eliminated. University education should be open only to those who can profit by it and have the necessary academic merit. For the rest, secondary education of diversified types that suits individual ability and aptitude should be provided. Therefore technical education and training at secondary level is of vital importance.

The Junior Technical School, a special type of secondary technical school, is designed specifically for students who wish to enter industry and other technical occupations. It offers a three-year integrated course in general education, technical education and technical training in various engineering trades. It accepts fully the concept of 'Double Finality' within its curriculum of educational development of the student from 14 to 17 and of his effective preparation for a definite technical occupation in life. In each year, general education, technical studies and workshop training are so integrated that all three elements constitute the base for the total development of the young student. Also, the work-load is so designed that the technical school functions as a cross between a factory and a school.

The workshop-training that constitutes over 55% of the total course and conducted in well-equipped shops provides a good foundation for the development of the student as a skilled worker of a high order. The development of technical skill is facilitated by training in engineering drawing and in elementary mechanical and electrical engineering included in the course.

5 Technical and Technological Education

A beginning of technical and scientific education

It is quite impossible to separate education in any particular era from the political, economic, industrial, commercial and social developments in that age and in any particular country. During the nineteenth century scientific and technical education gradually evolved and increased in importance, largely as a result of the political and industrial revolutions which has spread throughout Europe. Life and philosophy can change society: and society can change life and philosophy. Steam and electrical power did more than revolutionize modes of transport: they changed men's minds, the way they thought and believed. Mechanical devices in turn led to theological revision and uncertainty. The concept of evolution gradually led to concepts of control of evolution, control of life and death, increased control in agriculture, and control of disease.

In 1954 the Society for the Encouragement of Arts, Manufacturers and Commerce in Great Britain was founded, and in 1851, largely through the patronage of its President, Prince Albert, it helped to establish the Great Exhibition. Whilst this was acclaimed as a success for Britain and her industrial developments, on the more technical and scientific side it was clear that Europe was ahead. The lesson was, however, being learned slowly. In 1948 Cambridge University established a Natural Science Tripos; in 1853 the Oxford Honour School of Natural Science and six years later, in 1859, London University created a new faculty-that of Science, New Departments were also being set up in order to encourage more education in science for people generally. The Science and Art Department. The Literary and Mechanics' Institutes has also been developing since the turn of the century when Birkbeck left Glasgow to work in London, where he founded a Mechanics' Institute in 1823.

It was the comparative failure of British production in 1867, at the Paris Exhibition, that led to a Royal Commission on Scientific Instruction and the Advancement of Science. T.H. Huxley, who was a member of it, made a serious plea for science in the elementary school, emphasizing its educational value. Herbert Spencer provided strong pragmatic arguments for science as not only a necessary element of education, but virtually the essence of education. The Royal Commission, which reported between 1872 and 1875, and whose Chairman was the Duke of Devonshire, was asked to enquire into the state of scientific instruction and the advancement of science in the country, as well as the measures being taken for providing grants for this purpose. The report made a detailed survey of the scientific education provided, mainly at the universities and in higher education generally, but also in elementary schools, training colleges, grammar and secondary schools. It was obvious that, if more science were to be taught in this schools, more teachers has to be trained with scientific knowledge, and that the curricula of the training colleges has to be drastically revised.

The Devonshire Report found it necessary to insist that for every 200 boys there should be at least one science master. It felt, in discussing the aims of science teaching, that the he arrives by further observation or experiment.

It also considered that it was doubtful whether any other form of educational study offered the same advantages for 'training and developing the mental faculties.' However wrong the commissioners might have been in supporting the teaching of science on the basis of transfer of training and a faculty-psychology, they were right on more utilitarian ground concerning the need for developing scientific and technical instruction. They thought it highly important to introduce science into education at a very early stage; they argued that it was no more difficult to young pupils than grammar or arithmetic, and certainly more interesting. They considered, further, that, in public school during a thirty-five-hour week of study, at least six hours should be given over to science, and another six to mathematics; and they would not concede to the pupil the right to choose between literary and scientific culture before going up to the university.

The Devonshire Commission did not mince matters when it came to a final judgment on the national position concerning the teaching of science. They felt compelled to express the opinion that the general position was extremely unsatisfactory, a matter for serious regret; and considering the increasing importance of science to the country form an industrial and economic point of view, in the context of expanding European economics, they felt that its exclusion from the education of the middle and upper classes was 'little less than a national misfortune'. Professor Huxley, in the special evidence he gave to questions raised by the rest of the commission, argued that the separation of the teaching of science from education was like 'cutting education in half'.

The obvious concern felt by the Devonshire Commission was sustained both at the education and the industrial level. Without education interest in technical education it became increasingly clear that industry would suffer, and so there began a mushroom growth of all sorts of institutions with pretensions to giving some form of technical instruction. This created further anxiety that such instruction might not be properly controlled nor, in fact, be adequate to deal with the actual industrial and social problems. It was largely with these questions in mind that a Royal Commission on Technical Instruction was appointed in 1881, under the chairmanship of Bernhard Samuelson who has served on the Devonshire Commission. Samuelson was well qualified for the task; he has been a merchant and engineer, and a Liberal M.P. he was a man of wide culture with interests in modern languages, music, mathematics, science, and technical education. At the age of forty-seven he made a study of technical education in many European countries, and had already made comparisons with our own. He was a Fellow of the Royal Society and was later to serve on the Cross Commission.

The Samuelson Commission was to inquire into the technical and other instruction provided for the industrial classes of certain foreign countries and then to compare such provisions with that made for the corresponding classes in this country. The commission was also asked to consider the influence of this instruction upon manufacturing an other industries at home and abroad. It was, in itself, a considerable and searching exercise to set any commission, and without the spadework and know-how of the chairman over the previous fourteen years it seems impossible that six men could have performed the task.

The report itself appeared in several volumes during the years 1982-4; it felt, optimistically, that despite the progress of other countries Britain still held its position at the head of the industrial world; but

'In two very important respects.... the education of a certain proportion of persons employed in industry abroad, is superior to that of the English workmen; first, as regards the systematic instruction in drawing given to adult artizans, more especially in France, Belgium and Italy; and secondly, as to the general diffusion of elementary education in Switzerland and Germany...'

As a result of these contentions the report recommended that writing an rudimentary drawing should be developed as a single elementary subject, and that should be less part-time employment and more full-time education for children. The work of the Mechanics' Institutes came in for special mention, as well as a hint that many of them had fallen behind in their development of technical instruction. Many of them, however, has clearly seen that their teaching, both in content and method, was out model and unsuited to the needs and requirements of expanding industry. They were, therefore, revising their constitutions and their curricula.

Particularly praised for taking the initiative in providing facilities for artizans to obtain instruction in art and science, whilst their was more than a suggestion that the trades' union has a duty 'to promote the technical education of their members'.

The commission strongly supported the further development of technical instruction in this country , but it felt equally strongly that the 'Imperial budget' was providing enough. There should be greater expenditure by local authorities on this type of education, and they should be empowered to establish more secondary and technical schools. There should exist opportunities for intelligent young artizans to gain scholarships to such schools. Also, it was important that the great mass of the working class should be given those basic elements of the sciences which has some bearing upon industry. The use of the rule and the compass was essential to all, as well as geography taught as a branch of elementary science, more object lessons from nature, more dimple agriculture and more craft work. The commissioners took the view that men selected as foremen in industry should not be entirely ignorant of the more theoretical side of their work; and since they were drawn from the working classes the later, as whole, must be better educated in technical matters as well as in general knowledge. Similarly, when it came to the education of the leaders of industry, the commissioners believed that no part of the national expenditure on education was more important that spent on their scientific culture and technical training.

Other recommendations of the report included the provision of works schools in which young workers might be trained in the shops and factories themselves. They cited as an example the workshop school of Messers. Mather and Platt, which was a private evening school providing technical education for the firm's apprentices. The firm worked on the basis that the school must be brought to the workshop and not the workshop to the school; not only was this a simple and inexpensive way of training workers, it also had the advantage of providing the work atmosphere and brought home the immediate utility of the technical theory. Another recommendation concerned the training of teachers. If the children in elementary schools were to receive adequate tuition in technical subjects then teachers themselves also had to be taught more science and more art; this would mean changes in the curricula of the training colleges.

Form their general tone, as well as from more specific recommendations, it was clear that the commissioners were in favour of modifying the more generally accepted curriculum of the secondary grammar-type school. They were not opposed to a broad culture, but they were opposed to what they considered the dead wood of a great deal of secondary education. They were in favour of dropping latin and Greek and putting in their place more study of modern languages, mathematics, science and technical drawing. This sort of educational programme reflected very much the interests of the chairman and the general trend of educational thinking at this time.

A number of Parliamentary Acts as well as grants now began to assist technical education, in however small a way. The setting up of county and county borough councils by the Local Government Act of 1888 delineated certain areas of responsibility for the development of scientific education, and the onus for the further organization and establishment of technical secondary schools was firmly laid on local authorities. In 1889 the Technical Instruction Act was passed whereby the new organs of local government were empowered to spend a certain proportion of the rates on technical education and manual instruction. The local rates were further subsidized by grants from the Science and Art Department, as well as by the somewhat odd diversion of customs and excise 'whiskey money' to aid higher technical education. It was chiefly through such grants, and through the some-what *laissez-faire* attitude which inevitably arises when authorities are 'empowered' but not 'compelled' to do certain things, that the Science and Art Department appeared to be gaining more and more control of technical education, whilst the Education Department seemed to be getting less and less. It was for this reason that the Cross Report of 1888 had recommended that the responsibility for institutions which provided technical instruction should be transferred to the Education Department. The Education Act of 1899 finally created the Board or Education, which became a central authority taking over the educational functions of the Charity Commission and the Science and Art Department.

It is interesting to note, in passing, that despite the desire of the samuelson Commission to see the gradual extinction of Latin and Greek, the Bryce Report of 1895 boldly stated that.

'The classical languages are taught more extensively than ever, but less as if they were dead, and more as if they still lived, rich in all those humanities by virtue of which they have been supreme instruments of the higher culture'.

This report, most enlightened in many respects, saw no reason why classical and modern languages should not be taught together; and it applauded the growth in scientific and technical as well as manual instruction. It saw technical instruction as a means 'for the formation of citizens capable of producing or distributing wealth', and felt that an 'enlarged education' would result.

Whilst the 1902 Education Act represents a landmark in many ways in the history of the development and organization of education, it in fact paid very little attention to the pressing need to organize further technical education along sound lines. The science schools which had developed through the grants of the Science and Art Department were being gradually absorbed into the secondary system, or continued as higher elementary schools. Once the Board began to function it produced some regulations for the running of schools of art, art classes and technical institutions. These regulations, which appeared in 1903 and 1904, made provision for day instruction for suitably qualified students who might profit from more advanced education. These students were being prepared specifically for work in industry and commerce, and therefore such day instruction as they received would naturally be geared to the work of life. This was a theme taken up by the *Introduction to the Elementary* code of 1904, where it was claimed that the purpose of public elementary education was to assist the pupils to fit themselves both practically and intellectually for the work of life.

The *Regulations for Secondary Schools* of 1904 sought to distinguish very clearly secondary schools from technical institutes and classes which gave, almost exclusively, instruction and training in certain subjects to both adults and young people who had already completed a general education. Thus it was inevitable that the technical school should eventually emerge as a different breed of educational institution.

Junior technical schools

The junior technical schools had been under consideration and developing in a disorganized way, for a number of years. In 1905 they became a reality and had an immediate success, associated as they were with further education generally and with technical colleges in particular. The accommodation and equipment, as well as the staffing, of the further education institutions were profitably used by the junior technical schools; whilst, starting as they did with virtually no tradition, they were able to diverge considerably in curricula from both the orthodox higher elementary school and the tradition-bound secondary grammar school. Employers became immediately interested in these schools because of their vitally practical nature, and because they would obviously began to supply a superior type of youth for apprenticeship-one already trained in certain skills as well as possessing clear aptitude for the practical work of the factory or workshop. The various industries became sufficiently interested in this new educational project to make substantial grants towards their foundation and development, as well as providing staff to teach and train the pupils, and industrial equipment of very nature to give a sense of realism to technical education.

In 1921-13 the Board of Education published *A Report and Regulations for Junior Technical Schools* where by such schools were officially recognized as a separate category which in future would 'receive aid from the state to a degree more commensurate with their importance'. This was double edged. It was obviously an attempt to gain a greater control over the proliferation of educational institutions through the outside efforts of industry and commerce; it was not a declaration of the supreme importance nationally and economically of the expansion of technical education. The regulations established two main types of technical school at this time:

(a) those which prepared pupils for particular trades and occupations;

(b) those which provided an education to pupils who wished to enter a particular industry, but not a specific occupation in that industry.

In 1926 in the Hadow Report, on *The Education of the Adolescent,* there was the first organized attempt to define the origin, aim and province of the junior technical schools. Their chief purpose was to provide a course of instruction, extending over two or three years, for pupils who previously had attended elementary schools and had there received a general education. The curriculum of the junior technical school was designed to continue and expand this general education, whilst making provision for a special type of training for entry into some particular occupation or group of occupations. The committee felt that it was inadvisable to place a pupil of the age of 11+ in a school planned specifically to provide a course of definitely vocational education, and so the normal age of entry to such schools was fixed at 13+. They argued, as many have argued since about the whole question of the 11+ selection procedure, that the arrangement whereby pupils were given admission to junior technical schools at the age of 13+ considerably reduced the risk of committing a pupil to a course of study and training which might ultimately prove to be completely unsuitable.

From 1924 to 1928 Lord Eustace Percy, who was then President of the Board of Education, produced a number of surveys and reports on technical education, education for industry and commerce, and further education generally. A very thorough investigator, Lord Percy examined the problem from the side of industry and commerce as well as from the side of education. In the process he consulted something like 500 firms, and opened up enquiries into the field of special education for industry and commerce. He reported in 1928 that about 80-90 per cent of those undertaking further education in industry and commerce attended evening classes, and he argued that it was of great importance to develop day courses for such students, both full-time and part-time.

In 1929 the Clerk Committee on Engineering Industries strongly commended the work done by junior technical schools, and underlined the importance of recruiting for the engineering industry those who had received full-time education in them. By then there were 108 officially recognized junior technical schools with something in the region of 18,000 pupils, including 4,600 girls. The next year the Board of Education published its report, *The junior Technical School.* In this it was stated that the growth and progress of this type of school was steady, although not considerable. Each school had less than 200 pupils, whilst some had even less than 100; this was uneconomical, particularly when one considered the costly equipment used and the problems of staffing. Nevertheless, the report emphasized the serious-mindedness of the pupils under instruction, and the fact that their concentration derived from a sense of the relevance and practicality of their work. They were learning for life and this provided the necessary motivation to tackle their studies.

The 1930 report highlighted the real problem. The growth of these schools, like many before and since, had not in any

way been planned; and lack of planning in any sphere can lead to considerable wastage. The Board realized that local authorities had to be encouraged to work together in the establishing of more technical schools, and so it issued in 1936 its *Circular 1444,* in which it stressed the need for co-operation between neighbouring authorities when planning such provision. During the same year the Board published *A Review of Junior Technical*

Schools in England, a systematic survey of the way in which these schools were organized and distributed, the nature of their curricula, and their classification. Trade schools were included in junior technical schools, which now totalled 220; there were 41 junior art departments and 6 nautical schools. In 1937 there were 26,513 pupils in the junior technical schools; 2,366 pupils in the junior art departments; and 882 pupils in the schools of nautical training-a total of nearly 30,000 pupils in all schools which came under the general heading of 'junior technical schools'. During that year there appeared a Board of Education conference report on *Co-operation in Technical Education.* The purpose of this again was to impress upon local authorities the need to co-operate in order to pool their technical resources and prevent unnecessary duplication. The Board was determined to accomplish three things: the expansion of technical education; strict economy in this expansion; and the maximum of co-operation between industry, the staffs of technical schools and colleges, and board inspectors. It was suggested that joint advisory committees should be formed.

Secondary technical and technical high schools

The Spens Consultative Committee received its terms of reference in 1933 and published its report in 1938, which contained a number of recommendations about technical schools. It was felt that the word 'junior' in the name 'junior technical school' had misleading associations; and so it recommended that the expression 'technical school' should in future be used as a general term for all technical schools which recruited pupils at the age of 13+ and provided courses lasting for two or three years. The committee urged to establishment of a 'new type of higher school of technical character quite distinct from the traditional academic grammar school'. To effect this it was suggested that a number of the already existing junior technical schools should be converted into technical high schools, and should be given in all respects equality of status with grammar schools. They would recruit their pupils at 11+, by means of the general selective examination, and provide a five-year course up to the leaving age of 16+.

The committee felt that the curriculum for pupils between the ages of 11+ and 13+ in such schools should be, in general the same as that i other secondary schools of equal status, such as the grammar school. After thirteen there should be a liberal education informed by the spirit and practice of science. Subjects in the curriculum would include English, mathematics, history, geography, engineering drawing, practical crafts in the workshops, physical education and aesthetic subjects. In addition, some pupils would continue with a modern foreign language if they showed some capacity for profiting from it. Wherever possible these schools should be housed in the premises of technical colleges or technical institutes in order to make full use of the equipment and staff which these had. The technical high school would be organized as a department of the college or institute; and the head of this department would be the headmaster of the school.

The committee recommended that there should be a new type of school-leaving certificate for pupils in technical high schools on the basis of internal examinations. These would be founded on the curriculum of the school, but there would be external assessors, appointed by the Board of Education, who would ensure a uniform minimum standard of certification in technical high schools throughout the country. The certificates would have an equal standing with the existing school certificates as fulfilling the first conditions for matriculation. Finally, the report recommended that there should be close relations between the newly-created technical high schools and grammar schools, so that there might be ease of transfer at 13+ for those pupils whose later development made it clear that they were more suited to an alternative form of education.

The terms of reference supplied, in October 1941, to the Norwood Committee asked them to consider any changes they might suggest the curricula of the secondary schools, and also the question of any school examinations relating to them. The Norwood Report of 1943 largely supported the recommendations of the Spens Report, rather on the basis of a faculty-psychology which Dr Cyril Burt had already rejected in an appendix to that report. It argued that the relationship between local industry and the technical high school was an essential one which could not be maintained unless the school could freely control its own destiny. The report accepted a tripartite division of secondary schools, namely, secondary grammar, secondary technical and secondary modern, and opposed multilateralism as a general policy although it did not reject the possibility, or even desirability in some instances, of bilateralism. The technical high school, or secondary technical school, should give a general education, orientated from 13+ onwards towards special technical courses. Its chief function should be to provide a training for entry to industry and commerce at 16+, a training which met, at the same time, the demands of local industrial conditions. Facilities for more advanced work should also be offered from the ages of sixteen to eighteen.

In 1943 it was discovered, in the throes of a life and death struggle with Germany and her allies, that 'in the youth of the nation we have our greatest asset'. The White Paper on *Educational Reconstruction,* published in that year, recognized the need for some positive action if the country were to recruit more youths into industry and commerce through the technical schools, which it claimed held out great opportunities for pupils with a practical bent. It accepted the principle of the tripartite system laid down in the Norwood Report and set the general tone for further secondary development. The 1944 Education Act made it clear in Section 8 that it was the duty of every local education authority to make schools available sufficient in number, character and equipment so that all pupils, whatever their age, ability or aptitude, would have the most desirable form if instruction and education, including practical instruction.

The parity of esteem and equality of status, which had been sought so long for all forms of 'secondary' education, were at least recognized in law by the 1944 Education Act, even if they did not exist in fact. A great deal of hard work was put into establishing in the public mind this equality of status, but parents remained, and remain, strangely unconvinced. The Ministry Pamphlet 9, *the New*

Secondary Education, which appeared in 1947, maintained that the technical high school had become an integral part of the secondary school system by the passing of the 1944 Act. Because of this it had, at least in theory, equality of status with the grammar school; and, moreover, it came under the aegis of the new Building Regulations. With the invaluable help of the 'Ninth Body', i.e. the Associated Examining Board, which was formed in 1953, the secondary technical schools have developed a whole range of G.C.E. and other courses. Provision at the sixth-form level has developed with demand, and a greater degree of vocational specialization has now become available.

Higher technological education

In 1945 a Special Committee on Higher Technological Education, under the chairmanship of Lord Eustance Percy, reported on the needs of higher technical education in England and Wales, with regard to the requirements of industry and the contributions made by the universities and technical colleges. One of the committee's main considerations was the lack of liaison between the major technical colleges and the technological departments of the universities. Its chief recommendations included the establishment of regional Advisory Councils whose main purpose was to co-ordinate the technological studies and investigations in the colleges of technology, the universities and all other technical institues. Coupled with the recommendation was the suggestion that the Ministry of Education should establish a standing organization known as the National Council of Technology, which should give advice on national aspects of all regional policy.

It was further recommended that each Regional Advisory Council should establish an Academic Board to ensure that there existed co-ordination at the teaching level. At the same time adequate arrangements should be made for the representation of industry on both the Council and the Board, and for full consultation. The committee recommended that a selected number of colleges of technology should provide full-time courses of a university standard, as well as facilities for post-graduate work. Links with industry could be strengthened if industry released some of its more articulated specialists as part-time teachers. It was also envisaged that in the future both technical colleges and universities should educate students with a view to becoming senior administrators and managers in industry rather than concentrating upon the production of science teachers, research workers and pure scientists by the universities, and upon the training of technical assistants and craftsmen by the technical colleges.

The Percy Report further recommended that colleges of technology should conduct their own examinations and award their own qualifications. Courses of study would be approved and moderated by the N.C.T. through the Academic Board, who would also advise on equipment, accommodation and staffing. It was the function of the Board to ensure some parity of standards throughout the country and to select external examiners. There was some disagreement over the actual title of the qualification provided by the major institutions, but nune concerning its nature. It was to be the equivalent of a university first degree, awarded with classified honours. But it was felt that the institutions involved should not be grated a charter to confer degrees, l and the award was therefore to be called a diploma in technology. The Chairman, however, had reservations about this:

'If higher technological education is to be developed on the scale and with the intensity which we have been convinced are necessary to the well-being of the nation, it is natural to propose that such higher studies, wherever pursued, should lead to a Bachelor's degree'.

The Barlow Report, which appeared in 1946, was concerned with the nature and organization of the country's scientific manpower. It pointed out in general terms that only about 20 per cent of those capable of reaching universities, based on the level of their intelligence as shown by tests, actually went there. It underlined some of the conclusions of the Percy Report, in particular that university-type institutes of technology should be encouraged. Thus the number of universities should be increased and the output of scientists should be doubled. In the same year the Ministry of Education published *Circular 87/46* which accepted the main recommendations of the Percy Report and adopted a scheme for the reorganization of further education on a regional basis. In this way a close and effective contact between industry and education could be ensured, courses and curricula could be continually reviewed, new developments could be mooted and planned, and existing facilities could be expanded.

In 1948 the National Advisory Council on Education for Industry and Commerce was established. The Carr-Saunders Report of 1949 suggested that several defects existed in education for commerce. It was not based on a sufficiently broad study of the subject: it started vocational training, as distinct from vocational education, too early; and too much of the study took place in the evenings-there should be longer periods of full-time day study. With this in mind it recommended sandwhich-courses leading to new qualifications of degree standard.

The first report of the N.A.C.E.I.C. on *The Future Development of Higher Technological Education* appeared in 1950, and discussed technological education of first degree standard. The report recommended that there should be improvements in the financing of those colleges which provided such courses, and an improvement in their accommodation and equipment. It also proposed that a Royal College of Technologists should be establish, which would award associateships, memberships, and fellowships. In 1951 the Advisory Council produced a White Paper, which was a brief statement of the Government's policy for the development of *Higher Technological Education in Great Britain.* It stressed that in the university field the numbers of fulltime students in technology had increased from 5,288 in 1938-9 to 10,933 in 1949-50; and similarly the numbers of post-graduate students had more than doubled from 662 to 1,539. New building was in process. The University Grants Committee was encouraging some universities to institute post-graduate courses in particular fields of technology, including mechanical, electrical, chemical, agricultural and civil engineering, metallurgy, mining and textiles. The committee was also considering the possibility of establishing a university of technology for two or three thousand students, but the government was satisfied that it would not be in the national interest to proceed with such a project at that particular point in time. The proposal to arrange for the establishment of a College of Technologists was later reversed. The Ministry of Education's *Circular 255* of 1952, however, provided for a special grant at the rate of 75 per cent in respect of approved advanced technological courses.

In 1956 the White Paper entitled *Technical Education,* stated that the aim of the Ministry of Education was to increase by 50 per cent the output of students from advanced courses at technical colleges, and to double the number of part-time release students during the ay, thereby raising the number to 700,000. It clearly distinguished three grades of worker-technologists, technicians, and craftsmen; and it stated that the main road to the highest technological qualifications would be sandwich courses lasting four or five years with alternate periods in industry and technical colleges. It was expected that the scheme would attract pupils leaving school at eighteen, most of whom would be concentrated in colleges of advanced technology which would be developed from existing technical colleges.

In 1956 the Ministry also published *Circular 305, The Organization of Technical Colleges,* which delineated four main types. *Local colleges* provided, on the vocational side, courses which were mainly part-time and up to the level of Ordinary national Certificate or its equivalent. *Area colleges* provided, in addition to these courses, varying amounts of advanced work, mainly of a part-time nature and above Ordinary National Certificate and Diploma Level. *Regional colleges* were those which did a substantial among of full-time and sandwich courses involving advanced work. The standard of staff and equipment made it unrealistic to spread this work over too many colleges. Finally, *colleges of advanced technology* would provide a broad range and substantial volume of exclusively advanced work, including post-graduate work.

The terms of reference given to the Central Advisory Council for Education in 1956 were quite simply to advise the Minister on 'the education of boys and girls between the ages of fifteen an eighteen'. Part Six of the "Crowther Report, which was eventually published in 1959, was entitled 'Technical Challenge and Educational Response'. This section remarked on the need to produce far larger numbers of technicians and craftsmen. Among a number of recommendations made was the desirability of a greater degree of integration between schools and further education, and the need to transform what was then a varied collection of plans for vocational training into a coherent national system of practical education. Whereas only about 12 per cent of fifteen to eighteen year-olds were in full-time education, it was suggested that 50 per cent at least should be the aim. There was a lack of integration between school and college education, and it was argued that there should be expanded provision for 'college based' sandwich courses for young people aged sixteen to eighteen, provided satisfactory arrargements could be made for training in industry.

The White Paper entitled *Better Opportunities*

in Technical Education was published in 1961 and made some far-reaching proposals for a major reconstruction in the system of courses for technicians, craftsmen and operatives in technical colleges. The Government looked for a large increase in the number of students attending technical courses. It suggested a wider range of courses, an improvement in the methods of selecting students for courses, and more time for students to cover the necessary ground. There was an explicit desire expressed for more students to succeed, and for a reduction in the wastage rate through failure. Its chief proposals were that:

1. Student should begin at a technical college as soon as they left school, and preliminary courses in evening institutes should be discontinued.

2 The selection of students for courses should be undertaken with more care. The colleges should experiment with full-time induction courses and with tutorial methods.

3. Courses would include national Certificate and Diploma Courses for students aiming to become high-grade technicians at least; technician courses specifically organized for particular industries; craft courses and courses for operatives.

4. O.N.C. courses would last for two years and not three. Standards of entry were to be raised.

5. There would be new courses for four or five years specially for technicians.

6. New general courses would be introduced, which would lead to either technician courses or O.N.C. and O.N.D. courses.

7 Craft courses would be modified i various ways.

8 There should be a vigorous development of operatives' courses.

9 More time ought to be provided under day release schemes, and no student should have to rely entirely on evening study.

10 Sandwich courses and block release courses should be increasingly developed.

Thus, the White Paper sought to develop and implement some of the suggestions of the Crowther Report, particularly with reference to a greater variety of 'alternative routes', and a new form of full-time 'practical' education for those who were unsuited to the full-time academic route, or who would suffer from a wasteful part-time course.

The Robbins report and after

In February 1961 the Committee on Higher Education was appointed by the Prime Minister under the chairmanship of Lord Robbins; it reported in October 1963. In addition to the report proper there were five appendices in six volumes, and the total cost of producing it was £128, 770-just about £8,000 more than that of Plowden. Its terms of reference were very comprehensive, requesting the committee:

- 'to review the pattern of full-time higher education in Great Britain and in the light of national needs and resources to advise Her Majesty's Government on what principles its long-term development should be based. In particular, to advise, in the light of these principles, whether there should be any changes in that pattern, whether any new types of institution are desirable and whether any modifications should be made in the present arrangements for planning and co-ordinating the development of the various types of institution'.

(a) Institutions of Technology at University Level:

1 The volume of postgraduated study and postgraduate courses in both technology and science ought to be considerably increased.

2 There should be a major effort to encourage and increase in technological and scientific research.

3. In order that departments might use their resources to the best advantage larger institutions and faculties should be built.

4 A certain number of university institutions concerned in high level teaching and research, chiefly technology and science, should be selected for accelerated development. Financial support should be available for them similar to that provided for the Imperial College.

5. These institutions should each contain about 3,500-4,500 students, half of whom should be engaged on postgraduate work. Staffing ratios should be good, and adequate provision should be made for equipment and technical assistance.

6 It was recommended that the Imperial College, and the Collages of Science and Technology at Manchester and Glasgow should provide the

7 A fourth completely new institution should be immediately planned and a fifth should be developed from one of the existing C.A.T.s.

8 These two new special institutions should have an independent constitution.

(b) Colleges of Advanced Technology;

1 These colleges should in general be designated as technological universities, with the power to award first and higher degrees.

2 The Gratns Commission should be responsible for their finance.

3 Attached to each college there should be an academic advisory committee in order to supervise courses and examinations until the college was ready for complete independence.

4 Their chief emphasis should be upon the teaching of technology and science and in research in those fields, but the development of other subjects should be encouraged.

5 Each college should ultimately contain between 3,000 and 5,000 students.

(c) The Council for National Academic Awards.

The National Council for Technological Awards was established by the Ministry of Education in 1955. It was responsible for the award of the Dip. Tech., which was recognized as being of honours degree standard. The Robbins Report suggested that this council should be replaced by the Council for National Academic Awards which should cover the honours and pass degrees to students in regional and are colleges. More will be said bout the development of the C.N.A.A. Later; it is sufficient here to say that it was established by Royal Charter in September 1964.

In 1966, the Department of Education and Science presented to Parliament a White Paper entitled *A Plan for Polytechnics and Other Colleges*. This was an attempt to discuss and make proposals about higher education in the further education system. The colleges of advanced technology had now been transferred to the university sector of education, and the N.A.C.E.I.C. had emphasized the pressing need for further concentration of courses in order to achieve the most effective utilization of resources. The White Paper noted the rapidly increasing demand for higher education within the further-education system, and the fact that the Government believed the demand could best be met by establishing a limited number of new, strong centres with adequate staffing, buildings, and equipment 'needed both to achieve and maintain high standards and to provide the right setting for an active community of staff and students'. The Government considered the best results could be achieved by creating a number of polytechnics which would be comprehensive academic communities catering for students at all levels of higher education. In the appendix to the White Paper twenty-eight such institutions were proposed, although the final number was not precisely fixed in advance. Before a polytechnic was finally designated account would be taken of the possibility of associating a number of colleges by merger, or in some other way, in order to form the most effective unit possible. One of the proposals was to reduce substantially the number of colleges engaged in full-time higher education, but colleges which were not designated as polytechnics would continue to offer full-time courses of higher education provided they could satisfy the criteria for approval of course in force from time to time. Unless there were exceptional circumstances colleges not already engaged in higher education would not be expected to embark on it.

In January 1965 the Universities Central Council on Admissions reported that in pure science the universities would have admitted 1,080 more students if suitable candidates had presented themselves, and they could have also admitted 420 more students in technology. The Council for Scientific Policy was requested on February 25, 1965, 'to examine the flow of candidates in science and technology into higher education', and in consequence a working group was set up under the chairmanship of Dr F.S. Dainton, Vice-Chancellor of Nottingham University. In February 1966 the Group produced an interim report, and two years later, in February 1968, a full report. This made number of recommendations after stating that science and mathematics were, relatively, losing ground in the sixth form. The proportion of school leavers specializing in them had declined in relation to other subjects of study since 1960. It was clear that there had been an increasing preference for the social sciences, and the report deprecated this relative decline in technology and science which it regarded as 'potentially harmful both to individuals and to society'.

We cannot deal with the recommendations of the Dainton Report in any detail here, but briefly they included the following. It considered that in the sixth forms there should be a broad span of studies, and any irreversible decisions for or against science, technology or engineering should be postponed as long as possible. All pupils should, normally, study mathematics until they left school, and mathematics teaching should show some relationship to other studies, such as economics and the experimental and engineering sciences. The report felt that there was an urgent need to infuse into the teaching of science and its curriculum a breadth, humanity and up-to-dateness. It was the responsibility of schools and L.E.A.s to ensure that within five years of the report the majority of secondary pupils should come into early contact with sound science teaching. There was a great need, especially in science and technology, for the participation of teachers in in-service courses; and the development of teachers should ensure that younger and uncommitted pupils received high quality teaching in science. Positive incentives should be offered to an increasing number of graduates of high ability in order to recruit them into science teaching. The responsibility should be firmly placed upon L.E.A.s to recognize the additional costs of curriculum reform, and to be prepared to finance promising new proposals. The universities were recommended to look again at their entry requirements and encourage a broad span of studies in the sixth form and to increase the actual flow of candidates into science, technology and engineering. They should also experiment with new courses in these fields in order to attract into these disciplines able students who were uncommitted. Employers, in their turn, should recognize their own responsibility to ensure that careers in the areas already mentioned were made both possible and attractive to students. Finally,

> 'there should be continuing review of trend in subject specialization and their implications for manpower; research into career choice should continue; statistics on the flow of pupils from education through to employment should be further developed'.

The council for National Academic Awards

The Council for National Academic Awards received its Royal Charter in September 1964, and is a self-goerning body. It has the power to award degrees, which are comparable with those awarded by universities, to students who complete approved courses in further education established in colleges and other institutions which do not have power to grant their own degrees. By 1969 there were about fifty institutions providing courses for C.N.A.A. degrees, including polytechnics, colleges or technology, colleges of commerce, and at least one college of education. In September 1968 students taking C.N.A.A. Courses numbered nearly 16,000-full-time, part-time and sandwich. The C.N.A.A. degrees included B.Sc., B.A., M.Sc., M.A., M.Phil., and Ph.D.; B.Ed. was added to this list shortly afterwards. Although the officials prospectus lists over 190 courses being pursued by this large number of students, each college may, in fact, be following its own particular version of a course, provided its planning has been approved by the Council and it is examined by the Council's appointed examiners. There can be no doubt that the Council represents one of the strongest and most progressive academic forces in our society for the development of higher education, not simply in the fields of science, engineering and technology, but also in business studies, architecture, economics, languages, law, librarianship, public administration, social science and even education itself. The Robbins plan of October 1963, in less than five years from its inception in September 1964, mushroomed into an organization of colleges and students greater than any single university with the exception of London University. Within a short time its number of students will unquestionably be doubled. The members of the council and its many committees, as well as its examiners, include some of the cost outstanding names in higher education.

Technical and Liberal Education

So much has been written of the dangers of a purely 'technical' education that it may be necessary here to say something briefly on the other side. Technical schools, colleges and institutes, from the secondary technical school to the college of advanced technology or technological university, are all aware of the necessity of a broad, liberal education. In 1938 the Spens Report had stated that

> 'we are satisfied that it is the aim and purpose of the junior technical schools to liberalise every subject in their curriculum'

If the schools were aware of such a purpose at that time they have been made even more conscious of the need for this 'liberalising' influence during the post-war years. The Crowther Report of 1959 emphasized the need for a discriminating use of 'minority time' in the sixth-form curriculum for this purpose, and liberal studies have become the latest off-spring of the colleges of technology.

In May 1957 the Ministry of Education issued its *Circular 323 on liberal Education in Technical colleges.* It stressed the importance of the liberal element in technical education in order to develop in the student not only a broad outlook but also 'a sense of spiritual and human values'. The circular made the point that it was not just a question of *what* was being taught out also *now* it was being taught, and it suggested that less formal methods such as group discussions, seminars and project assignments should be used, and whenever possible the tutorial system should be introduced. In 1962 the Ministry published a pamphlet, entitled *General Studies in Technical Colleges,* which had in mind courses in technical education lengthened to the 330 hours per year recommended by the Crowther Report. In these extended courses there should be an increase in the time given to English and general subjects, including physical education. The students undertaking such courses would in the main by young men between fifteen and eighteen years of age, and when not attending college they would be at work in industry. The first need was to develop their communication skills, to assist them to make themselves understood in speech and writing, and to understand other people. To this end, the teaching of general studies and English should be regarded as a single operation, and each college should make the attempt to estimate its student's progress towards great fluency and accuracy in both speech and writing, increased clarity of thought and discrimination, and more awareness of the potential sources of information and a critical attitude towards them.

The Jackson Report of 1957 on *The Supply and Training of Teachers for Technical Colleges* had emphasized the need to introduce a more liberal outlook into technical education. The student must be enabled to see his own science or technology 'in the wider context of industrial activity and the economic life of the country and of the world.' He must also be concerned with moral problems, cultural issues, and the question of taste. To accomplish this it was important for teachers to process wide interests themselves, and to have sufficient *savoir-faire* to mediate to their students a liberal education.

The whole problem of the relationship between technical and liberal studies is well expressed by A. N. Whitehead in his *The Aims of Education and Other Essays*, in which he says that

> 'The antithesis between a technical and liberal education is fallacious. There can be adequate technical education which is not liberal, and no liberal education which is not technical; that is, no education which does not impart both technique and intellectual vision'.

6 Technical Institutions: Their Nature

Technical institutions in India at the post-school stage may be classified broadly into three categories viz. (a) those conducting post-graduate courses; (b) those conducting first degree courses; and (c) those conducting diploma courses. No institution, however, is meant exclusively for post-graduate courses. These courses are connected at certain selected institutions belonging to the second category where facilities for advanced studies have been specially developed. Institutions for first degree courses are distinct from those for diploma courses except for a few that conduct both. The general policy of the All-India Council for Technical Education is that degree and diploma course should not be conducted at the same institution. Underlying this policy is the need to provide full scope to each to develop in accordance with its own aims and objects.

The Junior Technical Schools, of which there are about 55 at present, are a separate class. Some are attached to polytechnics and some work as independent institutions. In the former, substantial economy has been achieved in buildings; equipment and staff. It has also been possible to establish a rationale between secondary technical education and education and polytechnic level. The two educational cycles can be gradually integrated into one unified system that takes off immediately after the compulsory schooling age of 14.

Technical institutions may be characterised further by the particular administrative authority, the Central Government, the State Governments, Universities and private agencies-that is incharge of them. There are institutions set up by each of these authorities.

Engineering colleges and polytechnics

There are at present 111 institutions for first degree or equivalent courses and 210 institutions for diploma courses. Except for the higher technological institutes at Kharagpur, Bombay, Madras and Kanpur and the Indian Institute of Science, Bangalore, which are in a class by themselves, al first degree institutions are either affiliated to universities or are functioning as departments of Universities and conduct courses as are prescribed by the Universities. The Higher Technological Institutes and the Indian Institute of Science, Bangalore, award their own degrees. The latter awarded till recently only diplomas and Associateships that had been recognised by the Central Government and other authorities, but since 158 the Institute has been empowered to award conventional degrees. The Madras Institute of Technology, another institution not affiliated to any University awards diplomas for courses in Aeronautical Engineering, Instrument Technology, Automobile Engineering, Radio Engineering that are of first degree standard and the diplomas are recognised by the Central Government and other authorities.

A majority of the institutions offer only the three basic fields viz. Civil Engineering, Mechanical Engineering and Electrical Engineering. The other fields viz. Mining Engineering, chemical Engineering, Metallurgy, Textiles Technology etc. are offered mainly by institutions that have been set up specially for the purpose. Historically, Engineering and Technology' were used to represent different fields and that distinction was reflected too in the scope of work of technical institutions. Engineering colleges were set up mainly for Civil, Mechanical and Electrical Engineering and separate institutions for the so-called Technologies. The distinction was purely scholastic, but the pattern set by history for technical institutions continued. It is being increasingly realised that the progress of technological education and research depends in large measure upon the integration of fundamental and applied sciences with engineering studies. It is also accepted that the establishment of separate institutions for individual fields is not only uneconomical but restrictive. The move is to have composite institutions as far as possible, or to diversify and develop the activities of existing institutions. The new institutes of technology that offer facilities in a wide range of subjects are cases in point.

Except for the Higher Technological Institutes, practically all technical institutions had till recently a maximum admission capacity of about 120 students per year. Some had even less. As compared to institutions in the U.S.A., U.S.S.R., and other technologically advanced countries, our institutions were certainly small units. Perhaps in the past there was no alternative. For one thing, the demand for engineers and technicians was restricted; for another, regional aspirations for technical institutions could only be fulfilled on the basis of smaller units more widely dispersed. Also, there was no Central planning and co-ordination of technical education that could have ensured general principles governing the size and scope of work of institutions. In course of time, however, it was realised that large-sized institutions were necessary to meet the increasing demand for engineers and that such institutions should function on a national level. The Higher Technological Institutes have therefore been planned for an admission capacity of about 320 students per year (or a total student enrollment of about 1600) at the first degree level. A special scheme has been drawn up and is in process of implementation, to expand the training capacity of selected existing institutions and develop them into larger units. Some of these institutions are now admitting 250-300 students per year. The establishment of 15 large-sized Regional Engineering Colleges has also been planned, each capable of admitting 250 students per year. Eleven of these colleges have already started functioning. Some polytechnics capable of admitting upto 300 students per year have been sponsored by the Central Government. The advantages of large-sized institutions are many. They are more economical and more efficient than the equivalent in small colleges. Nevertheless, their effect in to restrict dispersal of educational facilities over wider geographical areas, a factor of some importance in a large country like India. Out of this arises the problem, should technical and economical factors alone govern the size and location of future institutions or regional and local demands for technical education facilities be considered?

In any scheme of organised development of technical education, super-imposition is necessary, and institutions should be related to the needs of a rapid industrial growth. Nevertheless, as a people becomes socially and economically conscious, the store set by an engineer or technician increases and the aspirations of the people assume new dimensions. In such a situation, all legitimate demands for the provision of technical education facilities have to be met. The aim of the central Government in this direction is two-fold. A total view of technical education is taken in relation to five-year plans and no region or area is left without opportunities of advancement for its people.

Simultaneous with the establishment of higher technological institutes, and other all-India institutions, a wider geographical dispersal of engineering colleges and polytechnics is being deliberately promoted. The objective is that eventually every one of the districts in the country should have at least one polytechnic and that no State shall be without its own engineering college. The latter objective has been achieved in the last three to four years. As regards polytechnics, over 140 districts still require to have their own institutions. It is hoped that the new institutions to be established in the Third Plan period, will be located in these places.

Role of private enterprise

An important feature of technical education in India is the large role played by private enterprise. Of the

321 institutions in the country at present for first degree and diploma courses, 198 have been established by the Central Government and State Governments; 33 by universities nd 90 by private agencies. In quantitative terms, the institutions established by private agencies account for nearly 35 percent of the total number of seats and this is a very substantial part. A definite policy is followed by the Central Government to encourage and assist private agencies. Under the Second Plan, wherever a private agency by itself or in association with the State Government raised enough funds to meet 50 per cent of the non-recurring and 50 per cent of the recurring expenditure for a technical institution, the Central Government provided the balance 50 percent required as grant-in-aid. The Central Government also gave interest-free loans for the construction of hostels. As a result of this policy, nine engineering colleges and 23 polytechnics were established by private agencies during the Second Plan period as against ten colleges and 46 polytechnics established by State Governments and Universities. Private enterprise therefore constitutes a very important element of technical education in India and supplements in a large measure the efforts of the State. In order to ensure that the private institutions are run on the right lines and maintain proper standards, governing bodies, that include representatives of the Central Government and State Governments and the All-India Council for Technical Education, have been set up to administer the affairs and finances of the institutions. The same policy of assisting private enterprise continues under the Third Plan but the matching share expected of private agencies has been slightly raised.

Standards

Does the present system of a four-year or five-year undergraduate course after the Intermediate or Higher Secondary train adequately the type of engineers who could go in for post-graduate studies and research? Would it not be better to design a first degree course that aims at a higher standard of scientific and technological content and in which an adequate foundation is laid for advanced studies later on? Should the pattern of technical education not be flexible enough to permit of the training of different types of graduate engineers, and particularly of those who can become 'Scientist-engineers'? These are some questions on post-graduate studies and research that have to be answered.

Most people agree that a University would not be doing its duty unless it gave its technological students an education in scientific principles; that a graduate course in technology requires a knowledge of fundamental mathematics and science and that unless this knowledge is acquired upto a high level the student will not be able to turn his practical experience to good account. In addition, the technologist must have enough knowledge in his speciality to qualify for entry to the profession which, with increasingly rapid advances in modern science and technology implies courses in electronics, ultrasonics, servo-mechanism, nuclear energy and other new material that was unknown upto 10 to 20 years ago. Above all, it is urged in many quarters that the courses should be devoted to teaching the future technologist to be a leader of men, to live a broader life and have an understanding of the arts and sciences which make life more pleasant and the world a better place to live in.

It is hard enough for any university with fully developed faculties in the liberal arts and sciences and technology to live up to the objective of inter-disciplinary development and also to meet the challenges of new situations that arise out of the ever-widening frontiers of knowledge. In a normal engineering college, with limited resources, the task is much more difficult. Nevertheless, as an essential measure towards improvement, the All-India Council for Technical Education has recommended that every engineering college should have full-fledged departments of Physics, Mathematics and Chemistry equal in status and importance to engineering departments. The degree course should aim at a more fruitful integration of the fundamental and applied sciences.

Then again, the pattern of employment of technical personnel is changing rapidly. The old concept of an all-purpose engineer is vanishing and job specifications are becoming even more specific. The function of a technical institute is not to train a student for a particular job but to give him a broad-based education on which he may build later on a truly professional career in his chosen field. This education should enable him to fit into his field of engineering as a whole. Nevertheless, the pattern of education should be flexible enough to suit students of varying interests and abilities. It should also be responsive to the stimulus of change in industry and in research.

A majority of engineers required for industry and other activities are of a uniform type and can be trained in the present four or five-year course. The standard and content of the course in just sufficient to enable them to enter the profession. With experience gained in th field, they rise to higher levels of employment and professional competence. A limited number of engineers, however, is necessary for research, design and other kinds of original work. They constitute the sheet-anchor for all future technological progress. It is for the training of this small group, both at under-graduate and post-graduate levels, that special provision must be made in the existing pattern of technical education.

An important suggestion is to organise a selected centres a special three year under-graduate course in engineering, admission to which should be restricted to first class graduates in physics, mathematics and chemistry. The course should lay special emphasis on advanced scientific principles as applied to engineering. Such courses have just been formulated in Engineering Science, Aeronautics, Instrument Technology, Electronics etc.

Facilities for special subjects

Diversification in the field of training is an important aspect of technical education. As industrial development progresses, the need for personnel trained in different fields and possessing diverse skills becomes evident. As the areas of application of science enlarge, new technical disciplines are established which in turn create a demand for entirely different types of trained personnel. For instance, the application of nuclear science has established the new field of nuclear engineering and made it necessary for nuclear engineers to be specially trained. The application of electronics, transistors and circuitry to computers, servo-mechanisms and automatic controls has opened up new fields in which engineers ae being trained in large numbers. It is, therefore, a primary function of technical education continually to respond to new developments in science and technology, identify new technical disciplines and provide training facilities in them.

In India, the full impact of scientific and technological advances on technical education has just started and a marked diversification of the field of training is noticeable. New faculties are being added in institutions whose activities were till recently restricted. For instance, Mining, Metallurgy, Chemical Engineering, Petroleum Technology, Geophysics, Production Technology are some of the subjects in which several institutions are today offering courses. This is largely due to a definite demand felt at present for technical personnel in these fields for various development projects under the five-year plans.

School of planning

Among the facilities created for training in special fields, may be mentioned the School of Planning and Architecture, Delhi. The school has been established as a Central institution for the post-graduate training of architects, engineers and sociologists in civic design and planning, an activity of great importance to the country. The school also conducts a special course in Housing to provide the much-needed personnel for the housing projects undertaken by the Central and State Governments. A Department of Architecture has been added to the school, that conducts a full-fledged degree course as also a part-time course in the subject.

Management studies

Scientific Management is another field that has recently attracted considerable attention in India. And rightly so, since for the success of the numerous industrial and commercial enterprises that have been undertaken both in the public and private sectors, good management is *sine qua non*. The rapid changes that are taking place in the social, political and technological environment, are making it increasingly necessary for the modern manager to be specially trained for his profession rather than to come up the 'hard way' through the school of experience. His training is both a rigorous academic discipline, essentially educational in character and a practical down-to-earth mastery of tools, techniques and processes. Therefore, on the recommendations of the Board of Management Studies, specialised courses in Business Management & Industrial Administration have been organised at four selected centres in the country and it is proposed to extend the provision to a few more centres. The courses are essentially for persons the provision to a few more centres. The courses are essentially for persons who are engaged in management and have to be equipped to grow and for those who posses a minimum amount of practical experience and wish to enter the management field. In order that they may best serve this purpose, the courses are generally organised on a part-time basis. Two all-India Institutes of management are being set up at Calcutta and Ahmedabad for post-graduate training and research in the filed.

The Administrative Staff college, Hyderabad, established in 1957 as a joint enterprise of the

Central Government and private industry and commerce offers a 12-week course to young administrators from all walks of national life in the principles and techniques of organisation, administration and leadership in civil life. It lays emphasis on team work, and upon the basic fact that those who are called upon to work together will be drawn from different apprenticeships. The task is to make a co-ordinated group out of individual specialists. It is one that grows with each further step in technological development. What the Staff College hopes to do is to bring together young administrators from all walks of national life at an age when their views are formed but not fixed, to provide for the exchange of ideas to the common advantages and to promote better understanding between those in charge in different spheres of activities. The resulting cross-fertilisation of ideas and techniques will be of advantage to all who participate and to the community as a whole.

The different centres of Management Studies and the Administrative Staff College are complimentary to one another. The Staff College is not concerned with preparatory training. Is constituency is among men and women already expert but needing the opportunity to reflect, to compare notes and to equip themselves more full for their services. A National Institute for Industrial Engineering proposed to be set up at Bombay will be an important component of the Management complex that is gradually emerging.

Printing schools

For the training of technicians of the supervisory cadre for printing industry, four Regional Schools of printing have been established at Calcutta, Bombay, Madras and Allahabad. The schools, working in close association with industry offer National Certificate courses in the various branches of printing and each serves the States in the region where it is located. It is proposed to establish a Central Institute for advanced training and research in printing technology and allied fields.

In developing facilities for new or special fields, keeping pace with current advances is not by itself enough. To anticipate the future, to think and act ahead of the times is the challenge of technical education.

7 Technical Education and Research

It became imperative for the East India Company to produce technical hands to man the subordinate posts in various engineering activites. They first started Survey Schools for training surveyors who were required in good number for the Survey of India and later for the railways., PWD etc. The first Survey School in India was started at Guindy, Madras in 1774 by Michel Topping, the East India Company's Astronomer and Geographical Marine Surveyor. It offered a surveying course which also included algebra, mensuration, building construction and plan drawing. The institution was upgrated by adding a collegiate department in 1862. Other early attempts at starting technical insitutions did not meet with success. At Bombay the government started an engineering institution as early as 1824 but wound it up soon. Engineering classes were also started at the Elphinstone institution, Bombay but could not be continued long. In 1839 a Mechanical Institute was set up in Calcutta but this too was shortlived. An Industrial School started in Madras met with a smimilar fate. However, survey schools were doing a fine job. Roorkee had a survey school apart from the Thomsaon College of Civil Engineering. The present Bihar College of

Engineering, Patna also started as a Survey School in 1876 which was converted into the Bihar SAchool of Engineering, and further into a college in 1924. Now the new projects of transport, irrigation and building construction were creating a heavy demand for technical hands all over India. In addition to the Civil Engineering programmes, industrial and art courses had also been started in several institutions. The School of Art & Crafts, Madras had been set up in 1850 and the School of Industry the next year. Sir J.J. School of Arts, Bombay started with drawing classes when it was established in 1857. The Government School of Art, Calcutta was founded in 1865. Keshabchandra started a technical School at Calcutta in 1870 with the facilities for training in carpentry, watch-repairing, lithography, engineering etc.

In 1877 *The Statesman* received a spate of letters on "Young Bengal" which gave the impression that feeling was gathering strength against impractical courses of instruction. The 5 November 1877 issue wrote about the youth. "He is crying out now for Arts Schools, for Mechanics Institutes and he knows not well what; some kind of educational training which will make him, something better than quill-driver, or a mere talker and theorist.... He is dissatisfied with what he is, and thinks his education ois at fault". Later, it observed; "We wrote privately a day or two ago, to a high authority on education amongst us, to ascertain what his views were as to the wisdom and practicability of converting some of our schools into schools foe teaching the mechanical arts. His reply is now before us:

I do not see my way quite clearly on the question of technical education. I confess, But in my humble opinion, our University education is a sham. Our B.A. and M.A. are unable to think or write, anything; they have only a respectable amount of mathematics; no philosophy and no literature."

The reader must not conflund the two things noticed by the writer. As to substituting the mechanical arts, or what is generally called technical education, for the present school studies foe entrance to the University, our correspondent does not 'see his way quite clearly' but what he does see clearly is that our University education is a sham. In other words the degrees which the University is conferring in large numbers every year, are altogether delusive. So defective are the original powers of the native mind, or so unsuited are our educational methods to awaken those powers; or so defective is the University curriculum of studies or so imperfect are the University examinations that we are conferring year after year the distinguished mark of a university degree, upon a class of young men who are in no just sense of the word entitled thereto. Their attainments are confined solely to a representable amount of 'mathematics'. They are in no just sense of the word 'highly educated' or Scholars and the degrees conferred upon them are distinctly-a sham. It pains us deeply to believe that this is so complete a consensus upon the point amongst our educational authorities, that it is the truest kindness to the native community for us to direct the attention of Government pointedly to the matter. It is asserted then, not only that the education given in our schools and colleges is largely a mistake in its very conception, but that when we follow it right up to the complete attainment of what it aims at-it is just so much Dead Sea fruit. We are thus rudely awakened with a double shock. We are wrong at. both ends; wrong at the very start, and wrong at the goal. The education with which we are training the young is a race without a prize; the University degree at the close of it-a sham. The public is certainly not in a mood to let this last. If we are thus fatally wrong altogether, we must make a radical and complete change.

The position unforutnately did not change mucl Nevertheless, the growth of industries and engineering asked for technical hands and our education had to meet this demand. The Victoria Jubilee Technical Institute was started in 1888 to cater to the need for technicians in the textile and chemical industries of Bombay. Likewise, the Kalabhavan Technical Institute, Baroda was set up two years later. In the nineteenth Century four major institutions were set up by the Government in the four regions of the country; namely the College of Civil Engineering at Roorkee in the north, the College of Engineering at Madras in the south, the Bengal Engineering College, Calcutta in the east and the Civil Engineering College at Poona in the west. These colleges also had schools attached to them to train upper and lower subordinates (overseers, sub-overseers and draftsmen) for the PWD, Local Funds, Municipalities etc, Because Indian engineers and technicians were employed only in the PWD and similar government organizations, not in the developed industries which were exclusively manned by foreigners. It will be interesting to go through the development of these institutions individually.

Rcorkee University

This prestigious institutions was set up in 1847 by Mr. Thomason, the then Lieutenant Governor of the North Western Provinces, as College of Civil Engineering to supply the PWD and Survey Departments with Assistant Engineers, Overseers and Sub-Overseers. About that time the construction of the Upper Ganga Canal had been taken up at Hardwar and a big workshop constructed at Roorkee. James Thomason was anxious that technical manpower should be produced regularly and he thought that Roorkee was the most suitable place for starting a College. In his honour the name of the college was changed to the Thomason College of Civil Engineering in 1854. It was further changed to Thomson College of Engineering in 1847, and to the present Roorkee University in 1949 as a mark of its centenary.

The college offfered three types of courses; engineer class, upper subordinate class and lower subordinate class. For admission to the Engineer class an entrance examination was held. The students went through a two-year theoretical course, during which they received practicals in surveying and preparing projects. After the course students underwent practical training. Four or five posts of Assistant Engineers in the PWD were attached to the college. The report on "Technical Education in India" by A.P. Mac-Donnel, the Home Secretary to the Government of India, mentioned, "It is stated thjat some very valuable Engineers have been turned out of this college. This instruction in surveying is most through. They exibit great skill in managing native workmen and in applying the resources of the country."

The upper subordinate class consisted of students who had qualified in a preliminary literary test. The course lasted two years in the college and one year outside for practical training. In the lower subordinate class there were Indian students who had come through the preliminary test. Soldiers of the native army were taken in without the qualifying test. The courses of studies included mathematics, civil engineering, surveying, drawing and Urdu. The Engineers class had in addition experimental science and photography. The college also held examinations and granted certificates og qualification as Sub-Engineer, Overseer and Examiner of Accounts, PWD. A number of studentships were given. In 1886 there were a total of 142 students attending the various classes.

The college had no workshop of its own but students visited the well-known Roorkee Workeshops belonging to the local government. Since the students did not perform any manual labour there the visits were of little practical value. The report of 1886 recommended that the Roorkee Workshops be made over to the college and a system of practical training added to the theoretical course.

The colege maintained high standards of education throughout. In 1945 the U.P. Government appointed a recorganization committee with Prof. C.L. Fortescue as Chairman to examine in detail the working of the college in all its aspects and to recommend measures for recorganizing it on a basis that would make it more efficient, more useful and more up-to-date. The committee recommended inter alia introduction of undergraduate degree coursesin electrical and mechanical engineering, postgraduate courses in civil, electrical and mechanical engineering, and short-term courses in engineering development for the engineers of PWD, industry and members of the staff. It also recommended a four-year degree course in chemical engineering in conjunction with the Harcourt Butler Technological Institute Kanpur, such that the students would spend two years at each institution.

The college attained new dimesions when it became a university in 1949 by an Act of the U.P. State legislature. A faculty of Science was added with Departments of physics, chemistry, mathematics and geology and geophysics. New subjects in engineering also came under its care, like electronics and communication engineering, chemical engineering, metallurgical engineering and architecture. In 1955 the Water Resources Development Training Centre was started with assistances from UNESCO to train engineers from the countires of Asia and Africa in water and power engineering. A School of Earthquake Engineering emerged out of the civil engineering department and achieved international fame under the directorship of Professor Jai Krishna. The location of the Central Building Research Institute, Central Structural Engineering Research Institute and the Irrigation Reseqrch Institute at Roorkee proved to be of immense benefit to the university as well as to the institute in the programmes of education and research.

Bengal engineering college, Sibpur

First of all, a survey department was started in 1841 and a post of Professor of Civil Engineering was created at the Hindu College Calcutta in 1843-44. Professorship in experimental and natural philosophy had already been instituted there. Lord Dalhousie was keen that an engineering college should be set up at Calcutta as well as in Bombay and Madras. The College of Civil Engineering was started in 1856 at Calcutta with its temporary location at the Presidency College. The Civil Engineering Section of the Presidency College maintained its separate identity until it merged with the Colege of Civil Engineering in 1861.

The college offered a four-year degree course in civil engineering which had a strong practical bias. The students spent three hours daily in the workshop. Part of the final year course was spent on brickmaking, stone masonary, bricklaying, managing workmen and keeping accounts. Besides this course there were courses for mechanical engineers, civil overseers and mechanical overseers. These courses followed generally the outlines of the L.C.E. with appropriate modifications. In 1885 the enrolement of students in the degree course was 42 and in the subordinate or apprentice class 107. The principal of the college reported to the MacDonnel committee of 1886 that considerable apathy prevailed among the students even though all those who passed from the college or school found little difficulty in getting employment.

This was the only engineering college in the eastern region and produced many a great engineer. Situated as it was in the highly industrialized and most progressive part of the country, it maintained close contact with industries, government and Calcutta University. The courses were improved in order to move with the timesa. Aeronautics was included in the course as early as 1936 and degree courses in metallurgy and architecture were started right from 1939. Similarly, a postgraduate course in public health engineering leading to the ME degree was started in 1947 and in other engineering branches in 1953. At the university college of science, Calcutta communication engineering had become part of the applied physics course in 1936 from which ten years later emerged the new course in radio-physics and electronics.

College of Engineering, Guindy (Madras)

The survey school of 1794 improved its status with the foundation of a collegiate department in 1962. The name was changed to Madras civil engineering college and reorganization took place in 1885 after a prolonged discussion. The collegiate department prepared engineers for the degree of B.C.E. of Madras university but the course seemed to be wholly theoritical which was a serious defect. The average number of students in the degree course was 19 but applications for admission were more numerous than the accommodation and teaching capcity could meet. One engineer's appointment in government service annually was guaranteed to the college, "but still the colege is quite local in its effects, and the public workes department of the government of india knows very little about its results... The great want seems to be facilities for practical training, which having regard to the existence in Madras of large railway termine and workshops ought not to be insurmountable," observed the MacDonnel committee of 1886.

The school department trained students for the subordinate engineering posts. There were also classes for surveyors and draftsmen. The upper subordinate students got a year's training before appointment to the public service. The course of instruction comprised elementary mathematics, engineering, surveying, drawing and estimating, bricklaying, and the Madras Vernacular languages. There were 106 students in 1885 of whom 26 got scholarships. Applicants were more numerous than seats. The MacDonnel committee said, "it is therefore a matter for regret that owing to insufficient accommodation, all applicants for admission to the school cannot be received. An excellent feature of the organization seems to be a system of examination by which candidates, not being students of the school, appear and obtain on passing examinations certificates of competency as draftsmen and surveyors."

College of Engineering, Poona

The college originated from the Poona engineering and mechanical school which was established in 1854 for training subordinate officers of the PWD. The school was converted into the Poona civil engineering college in 1864 with a munificent donation of Rs 50,000 received from Sir Cowabji Jehangir and after two years it got affiliated to the Bombay university for the diploma of L.C.E., a 3-year course after matriculation. The college also offered courses in agriculture and forestry and admitted: (1) matriculated students studying for university degrees in civil engineering; (ii) matriculated students studying scientific agriculture in the college and the farm attached to it; (iii) matriculated students who studied forestry; (iv) students studying in the college and attached to workshops with the object opf becoming overseers. The student standing first in the L.C.E. was guaranted employment in the Indian service of engineers and six others, in order of merit, were employed by the Bombay PWD.

Big workshops were attached to the College which had been extended from time to time with theprofits made on works executed them. The University of Bombay required candidates for the L.C.E. degree to perform manual work before the examiners; and therefore a course of practical training was necessary unlikethat in madras. Overseers had to undergo a workshop course of a two to four year duration and it was they who chiefly executed the jobs in the workshops. In 1885, the Engineering College admitted 103 students while the Engineering School admitted 67.

This institution served as a college of science till 1911 and offered degree courses in a number of branches. Agriculture courses which had been instituted as early as 1879, later developed into degree and diploma courses. Veterinary education was also provided. Being the premier institution of Bombay University in science and technology, it always ventured into new fields. It started forestry classes too in order to provide rangers for the Forest Department. Perhaps because it was too much for the college to bear, the forestry course was dropped, followed by the agriculture and veterinary classes in 1911. In the meantime the Master of Civil

Engineering course had been started as 1890. The B.E. degree course in civil engineering was started in 1909, that in mechanical engineering in 1913, in electrical engineering in 1917 and in metallurgy and tele-communication in 1952. This was the only college in Western India untill 1937 which offered degree courses in engineering.

Of course, at the diploma or technician level the Victorial Jubilee Technical Institute, Bombay had been serving the region since 1888. The Government of Bombay resolution of 15 September, 1886 drew the attention of industrialists to the question of providing facilities for technical education in the City of Bombay new technical developments. Public donations were raised to which the Bombay Municipal Corporation added Rs. 80,000 which it had set aside for creating a permanent memorial to the completion of fifty years of the reign of Queen Victoria. The government accepted the proposal to estbalish a technical institute with the assurance of an annual recurring grant and so the VJTI was founded in 1888. It continued with the diploma courses until 1944 when it expanded its scope to degree courses in electrical engineering, mechanical engineering and textile technology. Later, postgraduate courses in textile technology and other branches including automobile engineering were also introduced.

Sir J.J. College of Architecture

Sir J.J. College of Architecture, Bombay is the oldest institution in the whole of Asia imparting architectural education. It was founded in 1896 on the advice of John Begg, the first Consulting Architect of the Government of Bombay presidency as a department of Sir J.J. School of art. In the beginning a draftsman's course of duration was raised to 4 years. The first Government Diploma Examination in Architecture was held in 1923.

A degree course in architecture was started at the Indian institute of Technology, Kharagpur as well as at the School of planning & Architecture, Delhi in 1952. It became necessary for Sir J.J. College to redesignate its course and give a degree in place of a Diploma. Hence the college got affliation with the University of Bombay. it was renamed as Sir J.J. College of Architecture in 1958. The budget for this college was almost stagnant at the level of 1958 for many years to come. The development of the college could not keep pace with the changing times and trends. The management of the college was transferred to the Bombay University in 1973, and the change created a better atmosphere for improvement in both academic and physical facilities.

Chemical technology

In order to meet the growing need for manpower in textile technology, training and educational facilities in the field were opened in several parts of the country. The government school of Dyeing and printing and the government Textile school were merged in 1937 to form the government Central Textile Instute, Kanpur. The R.C. Technical Institute, Ahmedabad, was set up on 1910. At Amritsar, the government Central WEaving Institute, later renamed Punjab Institute of textile technology, was established in 1920. The government Textile Institute, Madras was established in 1923, and the Bengal Silk Technology Institute was set up in 1927 at Murshidabad.

Apart from textile technology, developments were taking place in chemical and allied fields. in order to cater to theneeds of such industries, several institutions were started in various regions of the country, The Harcourt Butler Technological Institute (HBTI), Kanpur was started in 1920 for postgraduate education and research. A section in oil chemistry was set up at the University College of Science and Technology, Calcutta. A department of industrial chemistry was set up at the University College of Science and Technology, Calcutta. A department of Industrial chemistry, which was transformed into the college of Technology in 1939, had been established at the banaras Hindu University in 1921. The college gave courses in glass technology, ceramics, pharmaceuties and industrial chemistry. The J.V.D. College of Science and Technology, Andhra University, Waltair was started in 1933. It offered courses in pure physics, pure chemistry, applied physics and chemical technology, and later in the chemistry of food and drugs, pharmacy and chemical engineering.

The University Department of Chemical Technology, Bombay was started in 1934. Until then the State of Bombay, which was the centre of chemical industries, had no facilities in advanced technological education and research. That year a two-year postgraduate course in textile chemistry and chemical engineering was started at the campus of the Institute of Science. The Department shifted to its own building in 1943. Thereafter the scope was expanded with the addition of courses in pharmaceuticals and fine chemicals, intermediates and dyes, oils, fats and waxes,. plastics, pigments and varnishes, foods and drugs. The department is recognized by the University Grants Commission as a Centre of Advanced Study. The department actively cooperated witht he industries in carrying out research and development work on urgent industrial problems and also long-term industrial projects. Thus the department has made valuable contribution to the development of chemical industries in India whereby several industries have been placed on a sound footing and many new industries have been started. A large number of chemicals and textile industries in the country are headed by ex-students of the Department.

Several multi-disciplinary institutions had been started in the early twentieth century to cater to the needs of enginering and technological education and research. The most important of these is the Indian Institute of Science, Bangalore set up by the Tatas in 1911 as a Centre of postgraduate work in various branches of engineering and science. The institute gave courses in electrical technology, electrical communication engineering, aeronautical engineering, Chemical engineering, etc., initially for its own diploma and Associateship and later for B.E., M.E., degrees etc., when the institute was deemed to be a university be the Ministry of Education, Government of India under the U.G.C. Act. The Biochemistry Department of the Institute is recognized by the U.G.C. as a centre of Advanced Study.

The government Engineering College, Bangalore was started in 1917 by the great engineer-statesman

Sri M. Visvesvaraya. Another great institution, the Engineering College at the Banaras Hindu University was established by the Eminent nationalist, Sri Madan Mohan Malviya. it gave a five-year degree course in combined electrical and mechanical engineering which had a high content of practical training of a one-and-a-half year duration. The college merged with the College of Technology and the College of Mining and Metallurgy of B.H.U. to form an Institute of Technology in 1968. The Indian School of Mines, Dhanbad was set up in 1926 on the model of the Royal School of mines, London. It was deemed to be a university in the sixties under the U.G.C. Act. The Technical College, Jodhpur was founded in 1922, two more were founded, at Dayalbagh in 1927 and at Ludhiana in 1938. The Jadavpur University has its origin in the Bengal Technical Institute founded in 1906 under the national system of education, which developed into a college in 1928. The Osmania Engineering College of Engineering, Trivandrum in 1938. Before the Second World War the number of engineering colleges giving degree-level education mainly in civil, electrical and mechanical engineering was only 11. In other branches e.g., chemical engineering, mining, metallurgy et., the facilities were very limited. The A.C. College of Technology, Madras University, came into existence in 1944, the college of Engineering, Coimbatore and department of Engineering, Annamalai University in 1945 and the College of Engineering at Kakinada and Anantpur in 1946. The same year the Institute of Jute Technology was a set up at Calcutta with a grant from the Indian Jute Mills Association.

A preliminary report on the survey of technical institutions in India conducted by the All India Council for Technical Education (AICTE) in 1946 showed that the engineering and technical institutions were mostly conceutrated in the southern region, art and architecture institutions in the northern and sourthern, and commerce institutions in the western. The facilities for education in the following subjects were available in the southern region only: aeronautical engineering, highway engineering, naval architecture, internal combustion engineering, tele-communications, cinematography and sound technology, fisheries technology, navigation technology and printing technology; sugar technology was provided for only in the northern regin.

Post Independence

Consequent to the spurt in river valley projects and heavy industries in post-independent India, the demand for technical hands grew by leaps and bounds. In order to meet the increasing demand, industrial training institutes, polytechnics, colleges and Indian Institutes of Technology was set up at Kharagpur in 1951 by the Governmenta of India with a view to providing leadership in the field of technical education and research. Later, I.I.T.s were established at Bombay, madras, Kanpur and Delhi. Phenomenal expansion of facilities for technical education took place under the Ghosh-Chandrakant Scheme of the Government of India. Upto the end of Second Five Year Plan a sum of about 50 million rupees is estimated to have been spent on technical education. There was an unprecedented demand for additional technical teachers as also for the improvement of the quality of the existing ones. Postgraduate courses and quality improvement programmes were started in a number of institutions and Polytechinc Teachers' Training Instutes wee started at four centres in the Country.

The Birla Colleges at Pailani were merged to form the Birla Institute of Technology and Science which was deemed to be a university by the Government of India in 1965. The primary objects of the Institute are "to provide for, and otherwise promote, education and research in the fields of Technology, Science, Humanities, INdustry, Business and Public Administration and to collate and disseminate in such fields effective ideas, methods, techniques and information as are likely to train young men and women able and eager to create and put into action such ideas, methods, techniques and information. "Sri G.D. Birla said, "What do we propose to do here? We want to teach real science whether it is engineering, Chemistry, the humanities, physics or any other branch. We want to develop a scientific approach in Pilani, which means that there would be no dogma. There will be a research for truth. What we propose to do here is to cultivate a scientific mind."

Thacker committee

Coordination of technical education in the courntry was done by the AICTE which had been set up as early as 1944. The system of postgraguate education was placed on a rational and sound footing on the valuable observations and recommendations of the Thacker Committee. It observed that technical education had remained almost static for a long time in India as was reflected in the general lack of scientific and technical progress of the country. As regards the organization aspects of technical institutions, there was little contact between technical institutions on the one hand and the industries and scientific institutions on the other. The progress of industries and scientific institutions on the other. The progress of industry depends largely upon the quality of its technical personnel e.g., the standard and efficiency of performance, adaptation, creativity, inventiveness etc. A formal system of education provides the basic ingredients of the necessary qualities. The remarkable success of Germany in technology owes in a considerable measure to her educational system. As early as 1884 the German chemical industries employed 4000 chemists who had got formal education in universities. By the turn fo the century engineering was becoming science-based and it appeared first in the form of electrical engineering and chemical engineering. In modern times engineering takes ont he characteristics of science to develop into technology. The Thacker Committee recommended that the existing degree course in engineering and technology be reorganized so as to enhance their scientific content particularly in fundamental science so that the prospective postgraduate students and researchers may possess a deep scientific grounding in the physical and mathematical sciences. This would facilitate the bringing together of science and technology which is a requisite of modern engineering research. the Committee recommended the establishment of full-fledged science departments in the engineering institutions with full opportunities of advancement in their own fields, even to offer full-fledged coursesin sciences. As regards the postgraduate courses it recommended a standard pattern of two-year duration having contents of advanced mathematics, instrumentation, material sciences, advanced studies int he subject concerned and a project work with disseratin. All this had a tremendous impact on the quality of postgraduates engineering education and research throughout the country.

Engineering research

Research in Engineering is a relatively new and still unsound aspect of technial progress in India. An idea of R & D work form the beginning of the twentieth century to the sixties can be had from the number of papers published during the period by Indian authors: 267 in civil engineering, 429 in electrical and electronics engineering, 62 in mechanical engineering and 146 in chemical Engineering Technology. In the field of engineering, research and development work may not lead to writing a paper like the field of science. In the case of the former the main aim is to adapt or develop a product or process, and hence the engineer rests contented by putting the new development into use rather than caring to communicate it widely through a paper. As a result, many developments are confined and perhaps lost in course of time.

Hydraulics and irrigation engineering came first for investigation as irrigation canals were built in various parts of India. The Roorkee Professional Papers of 1863-66 give an idea of the work of that time. The irrigation system made headway in the beginning of the present century and so did the investigations i.e., design of canal systems, hydraulic problems connected with river training, flood control works, water power generation and also layout of ports and harbours, and prevention of sea-coast erosion. The nature of the research was empirical, testing of models being the sole criterion of selection of a certain structure. In the field of materials, research was undertaken on surki-cement which was used at Krishanarajasagar in 1889. In the twentieth centruy Lindley and lacey made some contributions to the design of channels. However a superb contribution was made by Dr A.N. Khosla in hydraulic structure design. he evolved a new design criterion supported by mathematical analysis and model studies with electrical analory. When river-valley projects were started in the post-Independence era, research was undertaken in hydraulies, structures, water power etc., in a larger measure. Besides the design and development sections of the river-velly projects, the Universities, IIT's and laboratories of the CSIR, State Government and Central Government have made valuable contributions to Civil Engineering Research.

In the field of electrical power engineering there was hardly any research done in India till 1950. Thereafter contributions came from the teachers and researchers in engineering institutions and laboratories of the State Electricity Boareds, CSIR, Central Power Board, Central Electricity Boards, CSIR, Central Power Board, Central Electricity Authority, etc. Most of the work relates to electrical machines, transmission and distribution, high voltage technology, switchgear and protection, servosystem and computerization. Besides, the areas of electroincs and tele-communication were explored very widely and intensively by physicists and engineers. In the field of ionosphee and readiowave propagatin a lot of important work has been done since the time of Prof. S.K. Mitra of Calcutta University. Many papers were written on oscillators, circuits etc., in 1954-55. Although work on transistors was done since 1950, the transistor circuits came in for intensive study only after 1962-63. Highly valuable work has been done in electronics, especially on televisions at the CEERI, Pilani and on computers at the Tata Institute of Fundamental Research, Bombay. The TV cricuits designed by the CEERI wee used for the manufacture of television sets by Indian industries, thus avoiding the necessity to import.

In mechnanical engineering research and development started in India in the early twentieth century. Most of the work relates to machine design, thermal power engineering and production engineering. The railways have their own Railway Research Designs and Standards Organization at Lucknow. The CSIR started the Central Mechanical Engineering Research Institute, Durgapur which has its branches at two other places. There is also the GAs turbine Research Centre at Kanpur as well as the aeronautical research laboratory at Bangalore which works isn close collaboration with the Indian Institute of Scinece. The heavy machines industries too have their own research and development units. A very important contribution to mechanical engineering was made by Suri who developed what is known as the Suri Transmission for diesel hydraulic locomotive. This may raise the transmission efficiency to its maximum theoretical peak of 95 per cent.

Early researches in chemical engineering were most pragmatic as they arose out of the typical nature of Indian raw materials, environmental conditions, adaptation of important processing methods, etc. The universities took the lead in the matter of basic research. But later on when departments of applied chemistry, chemical technoloty and engineering were established, they assumed charge of objective orinented applied research as well.

The CSIR set up the National Chemical Laboratory at Poona, which has all along been in the forefront of chemical research in India.

Not much work was done in India in metallurgy before 1952. The National Metallurgical laboratory was set up by the CSIR at Jamshedpur and it established its name by developing a low-carbon chromuim manganese-nitrogen stainless steel. But is contribution to magnetic materials and manfufacture of Alni, Alnico and Alcomax types of permanent magnets are by no means small. The contributions of the metallurgy departments of the BHU and IISc are also considerable.

8 Technical Education: Its Administration

The organisation of technical education in India characteristic features of the Indian Constitution and a strong bais in favour of central planning and co-ordination. India is a union of States that are autonomous in certain subjects that include education. The Union comprises 16 states, each with its own legislature and a government formed on the basis of universal adult franchise. It is, therefore, the primary responsibility of the States to organise, develop and administer technical education and training within their respective areas.

The constitutional position notwithstanding, the organisational and administrative set-up in many States was till recently unsatisfactory. There was no single department in the state government fully responsible for technical education and a variety of a arrangements existed. In some states technical institutions were under the administrative control of Industries Departments; in some under the Public Works Departments; and in others under the Education Departments. In a few states, Industries Departments and Public Works Departments performed overlapping functions. In ths same states, the Industries Department was in chanrge of others.

Each department laid down its own standards for the courses conducted by non-unitersity institutions under its control, held examinations departmentally and awarded diplomas and certificates.

As schemes for the expansion of technical education on a large scale were formulated under the Five-Year Plants, it was realised that a unified approach to the problems of organisation and administration of institutions was necessary at the State level. More important, when a large number of institutions, especially polytechnics were established in all states, in became necessary to ensure that the institutions maintained high standards of instruction, and their examinations were conducted by an independent body on a uniform basis. The All-India Council for Technical Education, therefore, recommended that in each state there should be set up a Directorate of Technical Education in the Government and a State Board of Technical Education. The State Board should include inter alia representatives of industry, commerce, universities, technical institutions and other interests concerned with technical education. it should prescribe courses of study for institutions not affiliated to universities, inspect institutions from time to time to ensure maintenance of standards, hold examinations and award diplomas and certificates. The Directorate, as the administrative agency of the government, should be in charge of the organisational and management aspects of the institutions. The recommendations of the Council have been accepted generally by all states, which have set up their own State Boards of Technical education. In most states one single government department is now in administrative charge of technical institutions. The establishjment of this new organisational set-up for technical education in the states is of great importance. it has not only helped in ensuring uniform standards on an all-India basis, but in associating various interests with the development of technical education and co-ordinating their efforts.

The concept of central planning and co-ordination has resulted in the Central Government's playing an active role in the development of technical education and training in the cournty as a whole. This concept is justified by several important considerations. First, in any system of planned economic development a clear perspective of the different sectors is an essential pre-requisite to action, whether at local, regional or central level. Second, when the programmes of economic development include large-sized projects for key industry, power, fuel, transport and communications etc. in the public sector, it is the primary responsibility of the Centre to ensure that the manpower required for the projects is made available. Third, on a national level, facilities for advanced technological studies and research can be organised satisfactorily only by the Centre, which has also to ensure that the institutions established for the purpose play their due role in the development of the country like India involves a heavy financial outlay that is beyond the resources of the states. The Centre, therefore, has to bear a major part of the expenditure both directly and as grants to the states. Fifth, the Seventh Schedule of the Constitution places upon the Centre the responsibibity for co-ordinating and determining standards in institutions for higher education or research and scientific and technical institutions.

In view of the above considerations, the Centre's role in technical education has a four-fold objective viz.

(a) to prepare an integrated plan of development of technical education for the country as a whole;

(b) to establish higher technological institutions, institutions for specialised courses and other institutions of all-India improtance;

(c) to assist financially and otherwise state governments, universities and other agencies in the establishment of technical institutions;

(d) to watch over the progress of technical education and to ensure the maintenance of high standards.

These are essentially in the nature of educational leadership which the Centre has to provide.

Council for technical education

The most important machinery set up by the Central Government to provide this leadership is the All-India Council for Technical Education, that consists of representatives of all State Governments, ministries of the Central Government, Indstry, Commerce, Labour, Professional and Learned Societies, Universities, Technical Institutions, Parliament and various other interests concerned with technical education. As a national body, the All India Council advises the Centre, the states, University Grants Commission and other authorities on all aspects of improvement and development of technical education. its functions include inter alia, the preparation of plans for the development of technical education on an all-Inida basis; to assess the requirements for technical manpower of different types and to suggest measures required to meet them; to suggest improvements in the pattern of technical education from time to time to suit changing conditions; to establish liaison between industry, government departments an other organisations, on the one hand, and technical institutions, on the other; to co-ordinate the activities of State Boards fo Technical Education; to recommend grants and other forms of assistance that may be given by the Centre to the states, universities and other organisations in the development of technical education. presided over by the Minister of Scientific Research and Cultural Affairs and with the Minister of Scientific Research and Cultural Affairs as its secretariat, the Council functions with fewer handlicaps than most other advisory bodies, whose relations with the administrative authorities are not so very closely knit and whose recommendations are subject to further examination. As a matter of convention the recommendations of the Copuncil are accepted by the Central and State Governments. The fact that technical education is not a controversial subject has facilitated the work of the Council.

For the correct discharge of its functions the All-India Council for Technical Education has set up a Co-ordinating Committee, four Regional Committees and seven Boards of Technical Studies. The Co-ordinating Committee is the Executive Committee of the Council and co-ordinates the work of the Regional Committees and Boards of Studies.

The importance of Regional Committees in promoting a co-ordinated development of technical education in the different parts of the country cannot be overemphasized. The vastness of the country explains the number and variety of problems of development that require to be examined in the light of conditions and needs of each region. Schemes for the establishment of new and improvement and development of existing institutions have to be formulated and implemented on a regional basis. A constant watch over the progress of institutions, spread over the whole country, has to be maintained and expert advice and assistance to them have to be provided. These and other tasks can be performed satisfactorily only through appropriate regional agencies specially set up for the purpose and working in close co-operating with local authorities.

The four Regional Committees of the All-India Council for Technical Education deal with the following areas:-

Northern Region: Jammu & Kashmir; Himachal Pradesh; Punjab; Rajasthan; Delhi; Uttar Pradesh.

Eastern Region: Assam; Manipur. Tripura; West Bengal; Bihar; Orissa; Andaman & Nicobar; Nagaland.

Western Region: Maharashtra; Madhya pradesh; Gujarat.

Southern Region: Mysore; Madras; Andhra Pradesh; Kerala & Pondicherry; Laccadive; Minicoy& Aminnidevi Islands.

Each Regional Committee consists inter alia of representatives of the state governments within its area, representatives of industry, commerce and labour, technical institutions, State Boards, universities and experts. Constituted in this manner the committees are fully representative of all authorities and interests concerned with technical education in their respective areas. Their main functions are:-

(a) to survey facilities for technical education at all stages and to make recommendations on the development of technical education, including the establishment of new institutions wherever necessary:

(b) to make a preliminary examination of any institution seeking recognition:

(c) to tender advice and guidance to technical institutions within the region;

(d) to promote liaison between technical institutions and industry;

(e) to assist the states and institutions in securing practical training facilities.

The Boards of Technical Studies advise the All-India Council on all academic aspects, viz. the pattern of technical education, duration, standard and contents of courses, admission requirements etc. They also lay down the minimum standards of instructional facilities required for the conduct of various courses by technical institutions. The seven Boards that have been set up deal with the following fields:-

Engineering & Metallurgy

Chemical Engineering and Chemical Technology

Textile Technology

Architecture and Town Planning

Commerce

Management

Applied Art and Crafts.

In addition to representatives of technical institutions, universities, industry and commerce, each Board has experts appointed by the All-India Council in order to bring to bear on the work of the Boards, expert knowledge and guidance in various fields. In the 14 years that the Boards have functioned, much valuable work has been done in formulating courses of study in various branches, on an all-India basis that have served as a guide to technical institutions. The standards of instructional facilities like buildings, equipment and staff suggested by th Boards have formed the basis on which the Regional Committees assess the requirements of institutions and recommend grants. The Boards have also advised the Council from time to time on specialised courses to meet the needs of industry and commerce and formulated various schemes for the purpose.

Thus, with a Co-ordinating Committee, four Regional Committees and seven Boards of Technical Studies, the All-India Council for Technical Education has become a most effective national body for technical education in the country. Recently, a Board for post-graduate studies and research has also been set up.

The University Grants Commission set up by the Central Government in 1956 is concerned with the co-ordination of standards and development of university education as a whole. Where technical education at universities is concerned as, for instance, post-graduate courses and research, first degree courses etc., the Commission acts on the advice of the All-India Council for Technical Education. This has ensured a unified approach to technical education in all sectors.

In the Ministry of Scientific Research and Cultural Affairs, there is a separate Division for technical education to assist in the formulation and execution of policies and programmes. The existence of advisory and administrative functions in the same organisation is a feature characteristic of the Ministry and one that have made for much progress in technical education. The Division has also four Regional Offices, at Calcutta, Bombay, Kanpur and Madras whose respective territorial coverage corresponds to that of the Regional Committee of the All-India Council. Working in close association with the state governments, and as secretariat to the Regional Committees, the offices are concerned with actual field work and provide the much-needed link between the Center and the States. Among their more important functions are making arrangements for the practical training of graduates and diploma-holders; keeping a close watch over the progress of development schemes approved by the All-India Council for Technical Education; providing assistance to technical institutions in various matters; ensuring the correct utilisation by institutions of funds provided by the Centre.

9 Planning for Technical Manpower

In a planned economy, the demand and supply of man-power are vital ingredients. Unless an adequate supply of the necessary trained personnel is ensured, the progress of development projects in any field suffers. Unless the projects throw up a sufficient number of jobs to absorb the available manpower and provide employment opportunities in an increasing demand and supply of manpower must be maintained at all times. That calls for an integrated and statistical approach to the problem of technical education and training.

Scientific Manpower committee

The first attempt ever made to assess requirements for technical personnel over a given period and plan for the necessary training facilities was by the Scientific Manpower Committee in 1947-48 soon after Independence. At that time, however, no five-year plans has been formulated. Nevertheless, the Committee visualized a certain level of economic development to be reached by the country over a ten-year period, 1947-57 and estimated he requirements for technical personnel for industry, agriculture, transport and communication, defence and other fields. Qualitatively, it also classified the personnel required into different categories of engineers, scientists, technicians etc. and indicated the level of their training in terms of post-graduate and specialist qualifications, degrees and diplomas. For supply, it carried out a comprehensive survey of the state of scientific and technical education in the country, the available training capacity of the institutions, the shortages existing in the instructional facilities and the scope of developments the institutions. The Committee estimated that the requirements for technical

personnel over the ten-year period 1947-57 would be of the order of 30,000 persons possessing post-graduate qualifications and first degrees in various fields of technology and 33,000 persons possessing diplomas. To meet this demand and also to improve the quality of technical education, the Committee recommended a number of schemes that include development of existing institutions and establishment of new institutions. A scheme was formulated for the institution of research scholarships for the training of research workers in science and technology and of practical training stipends to enable fresh graduates and diploma-holders to undergo a stated period of practical training in industry. Some of the schemes were accepted by the Central Government and were implemented. They were the forerunners of more vigorous efforts made in subsequent years particularly during the Second plan period to develop technical education.

Curiously, doubts were raised in certain quarters about the estimates of manpower requirements prepared by the Scientific Manpower

Committee. The critics said that the estimates were rather high and that the country did not need as many as 30,000 graduate-engineers and 33,000 diploma-holders over a period of ten years. According to them, the economic development of the country was not likely to proceed on a scale as large as envisaged by the Committee nor as speedily. later events have, however, proved that the fears were unfounded.

Targets for five-year plans

In 1955 i.e. at the end of the First Five -Year Plan, technical institutions in the country produced 4,020 graduates and 4,500 diploma-holders. The number of institutions increased to 65 for degree courses and to 114 for diploma courses. Their admission capacity also increased to 5,890 students for degree courses and to 10,480 for diploma courses. When the Second Five-Year Plan was formulated, a target on nine additional institutions for degree courses and 21 additional polytechnics for diploma courses was proposed in the Plan that would have increased the admission capacity to 7,390 students for degree courses and to 13,080 students for diploma courses. This was the order of development visualised by the Scientific Manpower Committee. There was no noticeable unemployment among engineering graduates and diploma-holders. Quite the contrary. Doubts were expressed and rightly so, that the training of manpower was not being geared to the needs of the Five-Year Plan and difficulties were likely to be encountered in pressing on with the development projects. In fact, an acute shortage of personnel was reported in certain sectors. The Planning Commission therefore appointed in 1955 an Engineering Personnel committee to make an estimate of the requirements for manpower for the Second Five-Year Plan, and to suggest measures to meet the shortage, if any. In its report submitted in May, 1956, the Committee estimated that for the various development projects included in the Second plan, about 26,500 graduates and 50,500 diploma-holders in engineering would be required by 1960-61. The supply from the institutions during that period would not meet the demand in full and the shortage in 1960-61 would be of the order of 1,800 graduates and 8,000 diploma-holders. According to the programme of expansion of technical education then contemplated, the admission capacity of the institutions would reach only 7,390 students for degree courses and 13,080 students for diploma courses by the end of the Plan period. The Committee stressed that unless efforts were made towards a much larger expansion of technical education than then contemplated, and the gap between the demand and supply of technical manpower bridged, the economic development of the country could not progress. The Committee recommended that the targets of technical education should be increased by 2,790 seats for degree courses and 8,220 seats for diploma courses by the end of the plan period. To that end, a number of new engineering colleges and polytechnics should be established in the country.

In consultation with the Planning Commission the Central Government decided in 1957 to increase immediately the training capacity of existing institutions by providing additional buildings, equipment and staff. An "Open door policy of assisting private agencies in the establishment of technical institutions was adopted. This gave a great impetus to the development of technical education as nine colleges and 23 polytechnics were established by private agencies. The plans of State Governments were revised in stages and provision was made for the establishment of ten new colleges and 52 polytechnics. Finally, it was decided in 1958 to expand technical education on a much larger scale so as to meet the demand for technical personnel not only for th Second but for the Thiro and subsequent plans. For that purpose, a special scheme of establishment of eight large-sizee Regional Engineering Colleges and 27 additional polytechnics was formulated and steps were taken to implement it.

The targets of technical education were revisec twice during the Second Plan period and by the no of 1960-61, the new target of about 13,500 admissions for degree courses and 27,000 admissions for diploma courses was nearly reached. If out experience in the Second Plan has taught us anything, it is that an integrative and statistical approach o the problem of manpower is essential. A certain measure of audacious planning for technical education and training yields rich dividends.

With this advance preparation, no serious shortage of technical personnel is anticipated for the successful execution of the Third Five-Year Plan. In fact, the supply will keep pace with the demand. For the Fourth Plan requirements, for diploma courses by the end of 1965-66. To this end, about 19 colleges and 80 polytechnics are proposed to be established and the existing ones expanded. The new include seven more Regional Colleges in order that each states should have a Regional College functioning on an all-India basis.

Right proportion

While on the question of supply and demand, the right proportion in which graduate engineers and diploma-holders should be trained, is an important issue. The proportion in which graduates and diploma-holders are required varies from project to project and depends on a number of factors viz., the nature of technical operations involved, extent of supervisory and executive responsibilities to be discharged by personnel at different levels, degree of mechanisation, instrumentation and automatic controls adopted etc. Nevertheless, on an overall basis for the entire field of engineering, a proportion of 1:3 of graduates and diploma-holders is generally accepted. Our institutions, however, produced in 1947 graduates and diploma-holders in almost equal numbers. That was very unsatisfactory. The position improved gradually in subsequent years and in 1959, the proportion was 1: 16. When the new institutions now being established start functioning and train additional graduates and diploma-holders, the proportion will reach 1:18 during, the Third Plan period. Even so, that will not be wholly satisfacotry. Therefore, one of the major problems of further planning for technical education is, how to bring about a balanced development of facilities for degree and diploma courses. This is not an educational matter only, but is related to the pattern of employment of technical personnel in industry, departments of government and other organisation demanding graduate engineers for positions that can be filled by diploma-holders adequately or entrusting or graduate engineers work and responsibilities that can be discharged by personnel with lower qualifications. In several organisations, higher positions are filled exclusively by promoting persons from lower levels on the basis of length of service. Since the higher positions require personnel with better academic qualifications, the tendency is also to prescribe the same qualifications for initial recruitment to the service, irrespective of the actual requirements of the different job levels. Therefore, unless the pattern of employment of technical personnel in many organisations is re-organised and the available technical personnel is carefully husbanded, the present imbalance will continue. A disturbing situation may well develop in which the value of technical education and training will be at a discount.

Another important measure is to create special facilities of further education for persons in service, so that when they wish to advance in their profession on the basis of experience, they could be equipped with the necessary higher training. For instance, a part-time degree course for diploma-holders, who are in service and possess a certain minimum amount of practical experience should benefit many organisations and also reduce the demand for fresh graduates from universities. Further, it will give a great incentive to the diploma-holders for better technical performance. The fresh graduates could be absorbed into positions where they are really required. Such a part- time degree course in engineering is being conducted at two or three centres but enormous scope exists for extending it to other centres where the demand for graduates in increasing.

Pattern of admission

The pattern of admission to different courses is closely related to planning for manpower. An interesting feature of the present pattern is the relative prominence of different fields of study, which is also an indication of the state of industrial development in the country. On the basis of 1959 admissions to degree and diploma courses, distribution of seats between the various fields of technology was as follows:-

Fields	*Number of seats* Degree	Diploma
Civil Engineering	4192	10210
Mechanical Engineering	2325	4570
Electrical Engineering	2329	4580
Electrical Communication Engineering	375	240
Mining	290	455
Metallurgy	239	10
Chemical Engineering & Chemical Technology	485	-
Aeronautical Engineering	30	-
Textiles Technology	282	311
Leather Technology	20	115
Architecture	285	-
Other fields	658	819
Total	11510	21310

Civil engineering accounts for nearly 40 per cent of the total seats at the first degree level and nearly

50 per cent diploma level. Next in order are Electrical and Mechanical engineering that enjoy equal importance. This distribution is not accidental. It is the result of the development of the institutions over the past 50 years in accord with the pattern of employment of technical personnel. Civil engineering has constituted so far the largest field of activity in the country, and in terms of employment potential it has offered the largest scope for graduates and diploma-holders. Due to lack of industrial development, particularly in manufacturing industries, Mechanical Engineering, Electrical Engineering, Chemical Engineering, Metallurgy and other branches have been rather restricted in so far as employment opportunities go. However, this is changing very rapidly. The future trend will be for larger numbers of mechanical, electrical, chemical, metallurgical engineers as the industrial development of the country in these fields progresses. Such trends are already clear and a stage will soon be reached when the demand for civil engineers will settle at a level not very different from the existing provision of training facilities, and the demand for other types of engineers will steadily increase.

In order to meet the latter as it arises, diversification of courses of study in the existing as well as in the new institutions has to be planned well in advance and adequate provision to be created to train in various branches.

10 Technical Education and the Training of the Technician

The term 'technician' applies to persons working in occupations requiring a knowledge of technology and related sciences between that of a skilled worker and that of an engineer or technologist; occupations at the technician's level may call for inspection and maintenance, detailed development plans, supervision of [production work, detail construction. Collaboration with the engineer is an essential part of the work of the technician.

Though the term 'technical education' is at least a hundred years old, the use of the word 'technician' is relatively recent. Its precise occupational meaning is still not well defined but the fact that occupational levels exist between that of skilled worker is obvious. In fact the gap s so wide that two intermediate levels are called for, which will be referred to as 'technician', originating in the industrial field, is now extended to denote a certain academic and social level intermediate between 'skilled worker' and 'engineer'.

Although not all industries need such a category, there are but few at present who have not taken some action to utilize a level of training below that of university or full professional qualification, if only because university graduates are scarce and expensive to produce. Whilst persons with this level of training are in great demand, especially in developing countries, the number being trained is never sufficient to meet the demand. The prestige value of university studies and the increasing financial assistance governments will provide for university students have caused the volume of technician training to remain quite inadequate for national needs. This lack is acutely apparent in the United States and has been so in Western Europe until recently. In the Soviet Union technical training for this level only just keeps up with industrial demands.

Some countries, in the enthusiasm of setting up their own often expensive universities producing only small numbers of highly qualified men, have tended to neglect the 'technician' and 'higher technician' levels. The intermediate levels of secondary education, and fulfill many of industry's needs as well or better than the professional graduate. The situation, however, is rapidly changing and this level of education is a present the expanding area of technical education.

There remains the unresolved problem of whether the education of a technician should precede his practical training in employment (as in a French *lycee technique*), follow some period of apprenticeship (as in the *Ingenieurschule* of the Federal Republic of Germany), or adopt a 'sandwich' form by alternating periods of college with practical experience.

Although they differ in method, each system has its merits and each produces very capable technicians. It would seem that industry would profit from the three varieties even within profit from the triple possibility of full, part-time and 'sandwich' courses. Each country must adopt its own system according to finance, potential co-operation from industry and the type of educational establishment available or contemplated.

Once of the most striking developments has been the use of the technician route of education and training as an alternative to that provided by the university. Only a small percentage, of 10 to 20 per cent, of the more gifted students reaching higher technician status and wishing to go further, have taken advantage of these schools. Possibly the greatest impediment to the development of technician courses has been adverse public opinion, which exists even those countries which have the greatest need for them. For many years the single system of higher education found it difficult to accept an intermediate level between the secondary school and the university. Schools with intermediate goals were regarded as second-best and their graduates as university failures. The fact that some technician qualifications could be obtained without having completed secondary education also mistakenly belittled their worth even though their ultimate level was higher than any secondary qualifications quoted. The idea that qualification as a technician might be used as a condition of university entrance with possible exemption from part of the latter studies has been so repellent to those brought up in the old traditions that there are still some European countries which have not yet given support or even approval to such a programme.

Likewise it has taken a long time in some countries to accustom leaders of industry to make more effective use of the technician grades and to recognize their capabilities. In the United States has been found expedient in recent years to issue brochures and other publicity material in support of the greater use of technicians. Even so in 1961 the United States was training three times as many engineers as technicians. All these difficulties and deficiencies, however, are now being rapidly abolished by the more progressive countries as the following national accounts will show.

Czechoslovakia

Technical training to levels above that of the skilled worker has long been in practice in Czechoslovakia, as in indicated by the year of establishment, 1707, of the institution that has now become the Czech Technical University in Prague. The technician level is provided for in several ways:

1. The secondary vocational school provides a 3- or 4-year course for those leaving the 9-year school which includes both specialized technical training and general education to meet university-entrance requirements. This school also provides a 2-year course specially designed for those who have already completed their 12-year secondary education, and then desire a complementary technical training for industrial or commercial employment.

2. The vocational school does no give complete secondary education but offers a 2-year full-time course of training in certain appropriate occupations, e.g., secretarial, horticultural and poultry-keeping.

3. The secondary school for young workers provides part-time courses for those who have completed the 9-year school followed by apprenticeship training, have qualified as skilled workers and wish to improve their qualifications and status. The secondary school for young workers also admits pupils who have not completed their 2- or 3-year vocational education, or those who, after 9-year schooling, ailed to take up organized apprenticeship but have al least 3 years' practical experience. These three grades enter at different levels in the 3-year part-time course.

Categories 1 and 3 of the above schools, whilst themselves training to technician level, also permit those who have obtained the appropriate leaving certificate to apply for entrance to university courses.

Secondary vocational schools

This range of schools is classified according to a schedule which distinguishes the main types: industrial, agricultural, forestry, commercial, social services; nursing and health, adult education and the cultural services; music, applied arts and industrial design. Each type of school groups together a number of different industries. For example, an industrial (technical) school offers mechanical and electrical engineering, chemical technology, nuclear physics, mining, geology and prospecting, power generation, metallurgy, printing, building, surveying, transport and communications. Each area of study offers various specializations which prepare the pupil for the various branches of the industry concerned, e.g., precision mechanics and optics, technology and mechanical equipment of foundries, food-processing machines and equipment.

These specializations, however, do not mean that the curriculum prepares the student only for a single or limited occupation for the greater part of the time is spent on basic subjects which adapt themselves to a wide range of occupations.

At the conclusion of the 4-year course the successful students may apply for entrance to a university, or seek employment in the middle levels of industry as technicians, planners, designers, maintenance foremen, etc.

Entrance to the secondary vocational schools is normally from the 9-year school but there is an increasing enrollment of students having completed their twelfth year of secondary school. In the latter case the curriculum is composed entirely of specialized theoretical and practical subjects and is completed by he passing of a second school-leaving examination.

Selection for he 4-year vocational schools is determined by the recommendation from the teaching staff of the 9-year school, an entrance examination, 1 year's prior practical experience, preferably n training, and the recommendation by the industrial enterprise where employed. These schools are provided with hostels where necessary. All secondary-school pupils in both general and vocational schools are eligible for grants, the amount of which is based on family circumstances but is quoted at 70 to 325 crowns annually. Other benefits such as reduced fares are also awarded. A nation-wide service of vocational guidance making use of national social organizations, as well as employment offices, is available to give guidance both to parents and to young people leaving the 9-year schools.

Secondary schools for workers

These schools link their curricula on a part-time basis to those of the apprentice training centres and schools. They provide all the instruction necessary for the completion of secondary education, thus opening up many routes for the educational advancement of their more successful pupils.

Although the foundation of these schools dates only from the 1959/60 session, enrolment has already reached 15,000 and is rapidly increasing. The course lasts 3 years for 16 hours per week, half of which is time taken from the regular work day and half from the student's leisure time. Some of the courses may be taken by correspondence. Such courses are provided both in the apprentice training centres of industrial enterprises and in the secondary vocational day schools. In both cases the teachers' salaries and teaching aids are provided by the district national committees.

Those who succeed in the 3-year course may, if they qualify, apply for entrance to the university for higher study. If they choose to remain in industrial employment, they qualify in a higher category than the graduates of the secondary vocational school, sine they have completed both their apprentice training and their secondary general education. They have an advantage in the selection of personnel to be trained as foremen.

The general secondary school

Although the general school does not concentrate on technician training, its new orientation has provided a basic introduction to various forms of apprentice training through the concept and practice of polytechnical education. Pupils work six hours per week in industrial, commercial or agricultural enterprises that are associated with the school. In the theoretical curriculum two hours per week are devoted to technical means of production. Manual work during the summer holidays is also organized. Thus prepared, any subsequent vocational training, either as skilled worker or as technician, is considerably shortened.

The works institute

Section 14, clauses 1 and 2, of the Education Act of 1960 provides for works institutes which 'shall provide further technical education with special reference to a given trade and the required general education for workers who have completed vocational or complete secondary vocational education and have had several years of practical experience. Courses of study at works institutes shall last at least two years'. A system is thus provided for up-grading to higher technician level.

France

The development of technician training in France has been so rapid over the past 10 years that even a brief study of the system becomes obsolete. The intensive acceleration of this form of education is intended to continue under the Economic Development Plan No. IV and to show a higher growth rate than any other aspect of the educational system. The following estimated statistics this clear.

Educational establishment	*Pupils (in thousands* 1961/62	1966/67	1970/71
Colleges d'enseignement general	630	824	866

Lycees classiques et modernes	822	1075	1154
Colleges d'enseignement technique	222	341	406
Lycees techniques	205	420	516
Total	1879	2660	2942

These figures do not include private establishments, or those pupils that may be left in *l'enseignement terminal,* the former *ecole primaire.*

The technician group (*lycees techniques* above) will thus form some 17 per cent of the relevant age group to which must be added the students coming from the *promotion du travail* courses. If the meaning of the term 'technician' is extended to include those students from the *lycees,* or *colleges d' enseignement general,* who do not proceed to a university but undertake some form of specialized training for subsequent employment, the total exceeds 50 per cent.

However, these figure are estimates and the present position shows a very serious deficiency. In the beginning, technician training was carried out in the former *ecoles nationales professionelles* which until 1920 were the aegis of the Ministry of Commerce. After 1945 these schools were supplemented at a slightly lower level by the *colleges techniques.* Up to 1954 there were only 29 *ecoles nationales professionnelles* in France, six of which were for girls. Under the Reform of 1959 both these types of technical institutions became *lycees techniques.* The intake age of pupils, once at 11 years, has been progressively raised during the past 10 years and when the reforms of 1959 and 1962 are completed will be raised to 15. The following are the different grades for which the students are trained.

1. The agent technique. Following the 11-15 cycle of lower secondary education the student may enter a 2-year course in a *lycee technique* to prepare for the qualification *brevet d'agent technique.* This qualification is the successor to the previous 'BE' series-*brevet d'enseignement industriel brevet d'enseignement commercial*, etc.-which had established themselves as suitably qualifying their recipients for junior employment in industry and commerce. The *agent technique* qualification is not awarded until after a period of practical experience and training in industry.
2. The *technician.* A 3-year course following the 11-15 cycle of secondary education provides training for the *brevet de technicien* qualification. This is the successor to the former brevet of the *ecoles nationales professionnelles* and is intended to provide for the *cadres moyens* or section leaders, and those fulfilling responsible technical functions under only a general professional leadership. Here, too, a period of practical industrial experience is a necessary condition of the award of the qualification. This qualification also affords access to the five newly founded *ecoles d'ingenieurs de fabrication* after competitive entrance examination. The *baccalaureat* is not a necessary condition of acceptance. The *brevet de technicien* combined with two years of industrial experience is sufficient for admission to the science faculty of a university.

3. The *technicien superieur.* The institution of courses in the *lycees techniques* for higher technician training is a recent development. The courses are not yet standardized and vary according to the requirements of each industry. THe pupils are recruited from the technician courses previously described, from the courses in general education *lycees*, from those applying for entry to engineering colleges, ad from a part-time courses of the *promotion du travail* organization. The qualification awarded-the *brevet superieur de technicien*-has been made the legal equivalent of the baccalaureat for certain subjects and is valid for entrance to a university or a *grade ecole.*

The students in these sections enter industry as high-grade technicians supporting the professional engineer. Part-time studies are available in some areas for promotion to the executive level or to research activities. The decree of 14 January 1964 defines the status in industry of the holders of the *brevet superieur de technicien* as well as the conditions of its award.

Upgrading courses for those in employment

The programme known as *cours de promotion du travail* provides, in the larger urban areas, a system of part-time study by which many of the qualifications for skilled worker and technician, and even the *diplome d'ingenieur,* may be gained. There are three main administrative organizations for this work:

The Conservatoire National des Arts et Metiers, founded in Paris in 1794, now has branches in 20 more towns and provides a variety of different courses at various levels. Some 17,000 students attend the Paris school and 32,000 study in the local branches. Apart from annual certificates showing completion of various courses there is the *diplome d'etudes superieures techniques* (*or economiques*), of which 280 are awarded annually at the *technicien superieur* level.

The Conservatoire also has the very old but restricted privilege of awarding the *diplome d'ingenieur* to those fulfilling their studies by part-time methods. Approximately a hundred such qualifications per year are awarded by the Conservatoire.

2. The Centre National de Tele-Enseignement provides a nation-wide system of correspondence courses up to the level of *lycee technique*. About 33,000 students are studying by this means for some form of technical qualification and of these 15,000 are in the technician area of achievement.
3. The Course de Perfectionnement sponsored by the Promotion Sociale programme provides for courses staring at the CAP level and continuing through the *brevet professinel*, the level of technician, up to the *diplome d'ingenieur* that is awarded by one of the universities or *grandes ecoles* now interested in this form of recruitment. About 31,000 qualifications are obtained annually by such means.

Federal republic of Germany

The technician grade in the Federal Republic of Germany has long been recognized as necessary for industry and commerce. Consequently, the *Fachschulen* and Hohere *fachschulen* have a long-standing reputation in preparing for the technician and higher technician grades. THe establishments known as *Ingenieurschule or Technikum* also prepare for the latter grade. A clear distinction should be made between the qualification of *Ingenieur* and that of *Diplom Ingenieur* gained at a technical university or *Technische Hochschule.*

The 'Ingenieurschule'

Entrance to the *Ingenieurschulen* or to similar commercial schools was formerly mainly from the *Realschule* (or *Mittelschule*), being the lower secondary from of education, r from a *Gymnasium*, Pupils leaving school at 16 with the qualification *Mittlere Reife,* enter training in industry with the status of *Praktikant*-a from of apprenticeship. After 2 years' experience-a period called *Praxis*-sometimes supplemented by 1 or 2 years of preparatory evening classes, the student may seek entrance to the *Ingenieurschule*, often done through a competitive examination. His application depends on local regulations and on the quality of the candidate's previous educational attainment.

The above method of entry is still prevailing one. however, a second method, *De Zweite Bildungsweg* (the second way), is now rapidly developing and in a few *Ingenieurschulen* more than half the pupils are those who have followed the *Zweite Bildungsweg*. This system requires that a student, after leaving the *Volksschule* at 14 or 15, takes apprenticeship training, gains a skilled-worker qualification (*Facharbeiterbrief*), acquires experience in associated crafts, and has attended a part-time day compulsory school (*Berufschule*) for 3 years and supplementary evening classes of 31/2 years. This system, leading to the *Fachschulreife*, is clearly equal if not superior to the preceding one.

The course in the *Ingenieurschule* is mainly scientific and technical, but it does include general or associated subjects- about 20 per cent of the curriculum-such as a foreign language, economics, aesthetics of design. The duration of the course, full-time, is usually six semesters, with some allowance made for entry into the second or higher years of the course for suitably qualified candidates.

Pupils in the *Ingenieurschulen* who receive a 'good' or a 'very good' in the final examination for the qualification of Ingenieur are eligible, between the ages of 21 ad 35, to receive a *Hochschulreife* although in a limited range of faculties only. The 'second way' through *Fachschulreife* and *Hochschulreife* thus leads from apprenticeship to full professional qualification at the *Diplom Ingenieur* level. The number of persons following this road from beginning to end are a small proportion of the whole and plans are being discussed to find means to increase their quota.

The *Ingenieurschulen* have their counterpart on the commercial autistic and social side. Advanced schools of commerce, agricultural institutes, industrial and applied art and industrial science schools are examples of the many forms of *Hohere Fachschulen*.

Not all apprentices are capable or desirous of pursuing such extended studies. On the lower technician level the fachschulen provide day or evening instruction. They offer courses in mining, technology, sociology, commerce and agriculture, each f which has its separate faculty.

The 'fachschulen'

The courses in the *Fachschulen* (as distinct from the pre-apprenticeship *Berufsfachschulen*) are intended for those who have already completed their basic skilled-worker training and their associated theoretical studies. Some courses require a period of further practical experience after apprenticeship as a condition of entry. The length of the course varies between two to three semesters with day attendance and six to eight with evening attendance.

One of the main divisions appropriate to technician training is that of the *Technikerschulen*. Such schools (e.g., in Nordrhein-Westfalen) comprise one or more of the following departments; mechanical engineering, electrical engineering, textiles, textile chemistry, chemical industry, electroplating. The schools may be public or private.

The final examination is for the qualification of *Technikes*, a State-recognized qualification maintained at a level which is approximately uniform throughout the Federal Republic despite the division into separate provinces (*Lander*) for educational purposes.

The teaching staff

The education, training and experience of the teachers for all these schools present a special problem. For the schools mentioned other than the *Hohere Fachschulen*, the staff is pedagogically trained in addition to having general education and university education. The first teaching certificate is given at the conclusion of the university studies, and the final one after 2 years of teaching practice.

The lecturing staff of the *Hohere Fachshulen* is drawn chiefly from engineering and other industries without special pedagogic training. Likewise the workshop instructors are recruited from the ranks of experienced craftsmen.

Statistics for attendance in are as follows: *Berufsschulen* with pupils, *Berufsfachschulen* with pupils and *Fachschulen* with pupils. In the last category, *Fachschulen*, approximately 49 per cent were concerned with technical, industrial or artisanal training.

The Ingenieurschulen including other forms of Hohere Fachschulen, comprise establishments with a total of pupils.

There are no charges for instruction in the *Berufsschulen*. A few of the Berufsfachschulen, the *Hohere Fachschulen* and private schools have tuition fees.

Italy

The training of technicians is provided for in the *istituti tecnic. There are several* istituti *of this type:* industriale, *for industrial pursuits;* commerciale, *for commercial occupations;* agrario, *for agricultural employment;* pergeometri, *for estate management;* nautico, *for marine work.*

The course is normally full-time and of 5 years' duration. Students apply at the age of 14 from the *scuola* media having earned the licenza, or leaving certificate of that school. In some towns and-colleges, there are evening course providing the same opportunities for study.

The 'istituto tecnico'

Several programmes are often available in any one variety of *istituto tecnico,* such as the study of mechanics, heat technology, electricity, aeronautics, electronics and nuclear energy.

The course-plan generally has 2 years of preliminary general study of a scientific or basic technical nature, followed by 3 years of specialized subjects, according to the line of study chosen. A specimen plan of study is given in Appendix III. The evening course likewise has 3 years of special study. At the conclusion of the course the students take the examination of *abilitazionc tecnica* which, if passed, gives the qualification perito with an indication of the speciality studied in the course. Holders of this qualification may, be offered employment at technician level in industry and public services. It also qualifies for technical teaching, but only in laboratory and practical subjects.

Formerly, the holders of the istituti tecnico diploma did not automatically qualify for entrance to a university or polytechnic institute, but the law of has now made entrance possible to the engineering, science and similar faculties. This was achieved by amending the course of studies in the istituto tecnico but students under the new plan will not be able to enter before although temporary measures have provided for a limited number to do so by special examination before that date.

Pupils who come from other lower forms of technical education are released from the first and/ or second year of the course. Candidates who have studied by private means are authorized to sit for the abilitatione qualification subject to their previous full-time education record.

The fees for attendance and for the examinations are nominal. The proportion of the post-age group entering these technical schools is remarkably high as shown by the following table.

The concept of 'higher technician' at a level not far below that of the professional engineer is not yet fully developed or even well accepted in Italy. Two proposals are under consideration to eliminate this deficiency: (a) the higher technician level might be a first-level qualification in the existing university and polytechnic institute courses, occurring after 2 or 3 years in the 5-year course: (b) the present *istituti tecnici* should provide such levels of qualifications as an extension of their present work. Some are already doing this and the first students, tecnici superiori graduated in. These extension courses in industrial physics and industrial chemistry have been offered both on a full-time basis for 3 years or on a part-time for 4 years. The full-time students spend two months each year in an industrial employment appropriate to their specially.

The Netherlands

There are two types of schools which train technicians in the Netherlands: *the* uitgebreid technische school *for the middlelevel technicians, and the* hogere technische school *training middle-to higher-level technicians.*

The system is based on full-time attendance but part-time, usually evening attendance, is gradually developing, especially for the HTS. For the past 10 years a limited number of leavers from the HTS have continued their education at the *technische hogeschool,* thus opening up the possibilities of 'a second way' in the Netherlands.

The Uitgebreid technische school

The purpose of the UTS is to provide for the essential mediumlevel trained personnel of industry: draughtsmen, draughtsmen-designers, assistant stress calculators, foremen, overseers, assistant mangers. In addition, they train future managers of smaller businesses and trades, and personnel for whom a basic knowledge of technology is necessary although it will not be their profession.

The 3-year period is sometimes preceded by a 1-year preparatory class which accepts leavers from the ULO, the LTS or from the third year of the gymnasium or HBS. This preparatory year brings the standard of general education up to an acceptable standard as the basis for subsequent technical studies.

The UTS accepts the leavers from the LTS at the age of15 who have done well in the lower technical school and who desire further education and training. As a means of selection, an entrance examination is required. The course of instruction covers 3 years, of which one, usually the third, is spent in the industry itself.

The UTS schools teach not only engineering, but also the fine arts, design, painting, sculpture, advertising, navigation, marine engineering, aeronautics, etc. This middle-level technical education is retained in the reform plan now pending, together with similar education for girls in domestic and agricultural-domestic occupations and for middle-level commercial employment.

The 'Hogere technische school'

This type of institution, aiming at the upper-middle to higher-technician level, trains personnel who will be the link between management and production, or who will become the managers of small industrial concerns. Since 1952, it has been possible to continue with higher studies in the *technische hogeschool* after completion of the HTS. In practice only 5 per cent of the leavers go on to the technische hogeschool and they make up only about 8 per cent of the hogeschool student body.

Admission is normally at the age of 16 from the ULO school with diploma B, or after completing a 3year course in the HBS or a 4-year course in the *gymnasium*. In addition, a good pass in the final examination of the UTS is also sufficient for admission. Previous education to higher levels may exempt the student from the first year.

The normal course extends over 4 years, of which the third year is a supervised year spent in industry. The course covers a number of general subjects, basic scientific theory, special technical theory appropriate to the programme of study, and practical works.

As part of the total reform, admission requirements have been increased as from the school year 1965/66: entry is now possible after 5 year' education in the HBS, or 6 years' education in the *gymnasium*, and the length of the course may be varied between 2 and 4 years to suit the needs of different fields of occupation. The full 'higher technician' level, which might ccrrespond to a mid-way point in university studies, such as the first degree of American studies, does not exist in the Netherlands. The gap between HTS qualification and full professional qualification after 5-7 years of study at the hogeschool is therefore very wide.

The HTS type of course has also been reproduced and offered on an evening basis. In this case, the entire course lasts 6 years, and the student is required to be employed in work related to the subject he is studying. He is encouraged to get practical workshop experience during the early years and experience in the drawing or design offices towards the final years.

During the week 16 lessons of 50 minutes each must be attended, totalling 13.5 hours, between the hours of 6 pm. and 10.30 pm. This reproduces in 6 years the same amount of instruction as is given in 3 years of day attendance-the year's experience in industry for day-students is not, of course, required for those already in employment.

There are 23 such HTS in all. They have been slowly but steadily increasing in number with the result that 10,615 students were in full-time attendance in 1963, gaining 1,871 diploma of which 30 per cent were in mechanical, 14 per cent in electrical and 18 per cent in civil engineering. The figures for evening attendance are much lower, representing about one-seventh of the figures quoted for day attendance.

Sweden

The technician level of training in Sweden is at present the subject of much reform and discussion.

The two institutions most concerned-the *tekniskt gymnasium* and the fackskola- have been under review by the Royal Commissions, whose reports were published in 1963. If these recommendations are put into effect as expected, a very satisfactory and modern system will be created.

The Tekniskt Gymnasium

The tekniskt gymnasium still has only a fifth of the enrolment of the general gymnasium and can be entered only by those having a realskola or grundskola certificate. Two months of practical experience is also usually required before entry and an additional four months accomplished during the summer vacation before leaving. The course lasts 3 years and terminates with the qualification *ingenjorsexamen.* This diploma gives a nominal right of entrance to the tekniska hugskola. However, owing to the pressure of technical subjects and workshop training, it has become increasingly difficult to maintain the standard of the general educational subjects and, for that reason, candidates for the university are more numerous and more successful from the general gymnasium.

The proposals of the Reform Commissions will therefore give the technical *gymnasium* a 4-year course, whilst maintaining the scientific, economic, social and humanistic programmes at 2 years.

The new technical gymnasium will provide four main programmes: mechanics, electricity, construction and chemistry, construction will divide after the first year into domestic and municipal installations, likewise electricity into the studies of heavy and light current. All the technical courses will have a common core of subjects.

The necessary practical works experience has hitherto been obtained on industrial premises. The growth of these technical gymnasiums together with the fackskolor will make this kind of instruction difficult, or impossible, to attain in sufficient quantity. It is intended, therefore, to provide school workshop practice in the first 2 years, but to arrange for two six-week periods of on-site training at the end of the third and fourth years.

It is hoped that these reforms will raise the yearly output to 7,000 *gymnasieingenjorer* with more than 5,000 entering employment directly as middle-level technicians. The remainder may proceed to higher studies in the university and eventually gain the full *civilingenjor* qualification.

The 'Fackskola'

The existing *fackskola* for technical pursuits is in effect a variant of the *tekniskt gymnasium*. In its full-time form, it provides a 2 year course, and requires 2 years of previous practical experience. In its part-time form the course usually takes 3 or 4 years, but only two months of previous practical experience are required. Entry requirements are at much the same level as the *tekniskt gymnasium*, except that foreign languages are not required. The course is more specialized, has fewer general subjects, and can therefore be kept shorter.

The qualification gained, *fackskoleingenjor*, is technically equal to the *gymnasieingenjor* but in fact does not meet the requirements for entry to a university. Recent reforms have, however, provided the possibility of gaining the full *ingenjorsexamen* by independent study following the *fackskola* qualification.

The new reform proposals for the *fackskola* give this type of institution a wider though slightly inferior place in the Swedish educational system. It is intended by the late 1970s that 80 per cent of Swedish youth will continue after the age of 16 in either a *gymnasium* or a *fackskola*.

The future *fackskolor*, some of which were already being experimented in 1963, will have three main divisions rather than the four proposed by the act of 1962: *social fackskola, ekonomisk fackskola* and *teknisk fackskola*. Only the last is further described here.

The technical *fackskola* will provide four programmes: mechanics, electricity, construction and chemistry. For all these, there will be a common core of or technical subjects with special technologies varied to suit the option chosen. Both the construction and electricity programme divide into specialities in the second year.

Admission will be open to all suitable candidates coming from the *grundskola* with no entrance examination. Alternatively, skilled worker training may be acquired first and entry made later to the *fackskola*. For those who enter directly from the *grundskola*, a year of practical works experience will be required between the first and second years of the course. Successful completion of the whole course will be recorded by a certificate indicating the speciality, the subjects followed and the grades received. The more successful pupils of the *fackskola* will be enabled after the second year to transfer to the *gymnasium* in a corresponding programme of study and in the appropriate year of the corresponding courses. These *fackskolor* will produce the junior technicians of the Swedish system.

At present the junior technician levels are covered by the *tekniska skolor*. Admission in the day course is at 16/17 after six months of practical experience, and in the evening courses at 15/16. The first level course is for the qualification of *tekniker*, lasting 1.5 years by day or 2 years by evening classes. Exemption from the work done in the first two semesters is sometimes given depending on the student's previous training. This level of qualification can be raised by subsequent attendance in more advanced technical courses.

In the major cities there is a more advanced institution which, admitting after the school-leaving examination, leads by way of the *tekniker* level to a further grade known as *institutsingenjor*. The duration of study is two terms by day, or four terms by evening study, after reaching the *tekniker* level.

These institutions and their degrees will be diminished in scope and purpose as the *fackskola* system develops in order to avoid overlapping. A conversion of the *tekniska skolor* to the *fackskola* system can be anticipated.

The new *fackskola* organization is developing and is expected to continue as shown by the following percentages:

The two main levels of technician qualification in the new system will be as follows: at the conclusion of the new *fackskola* with a diploma approximating the present *institutsingenjor*, at the conclusion of the new *tekniskt gymnasium* which, by reason of its 4-year course, should reach a technical level equivalent or superior to that of the present *gymnasieingenjor*. Beyond this is the *civilingenjor*-the full professional qualification of engineer-obtainable only by full-time university studies.

Union of soviet socialist republics

The 'Technicum'

The specialized secondary education offered in *technicums* and in similar colleges is an integral part of the Soviet educational system. It gives a programme of specialized secondary education, combined with the completion of full general secondary education.

In 1917 there were 450 such colleges having 54,000 students. At the present time there are 3.600 *technicums* and similar colleges with 3 million students. The education and training given are essentially for the middle-level technician personnel in industry, construction, agriculture, transport, etc. Specialized secondary education also covers pedagogy, the arts and para-medicine.

In the technical and the agricultural programmes the students obtain not only a technical and the agricultural programmes the students skilled worker training in a craft associated with the intended technician occupation.

The duration of studies in a *technicum* varies between 3 and 5 years for those who enter after 8-years schooling and from 1.5 to 3 years for those who have completed their full secondary education. Examples of both types are given in Appendix III.

Full-time attendance is the usual system but for those engaged in productive employment, there are correspondence and evening courses available through extension courses of regular universities or through institutes founded for that purpose.

Tuition in the *technicums* and in the majority of educational institutions is free and, in addition, facilities and grants are available to the students. In the day departments students successfully attending a *technicum* receive a yearly stipend and those whose homes are at a distance also receive a living allowance. Necessary journeys to the factory, farm, or other place of practical instruction are also paid. The external students who are employed while following a *technicum* course benefit from the following facilities.

1. They receive additional leave with pay for laboratory work and test examinations. With the evening courses, this amounts to 10 calendar days per year, for the first and second years of the course, and with correspondence courses to 30 days per year. In the third and subsequent years of the course, these figures increases to 20 and 40 respectively. Additional unpaid leave is granted during the state examinations for a period up to 30 days and for the diploma project for a period up to two months.

2. They are paid for the time spent in laboratory and practical work or examinations, and reimbursed 50 per cent of the cost of the journey from the place of residence to the college and return.

3. In the final years of the evening or external forms of study, up to one month's leave without pay may be granted to permit the student to

become acquainted with the leading industries in his specialization.

The entrance examination, open to all students, includes a test in the use of the mother tongue, mathematics and other subjects appropriates to the specialization concerned. In the day departments, the age limit is 30, but in the external and evening sections there is no age limit. The committees which make the final selection of entrants are composed of academic staff and of officials of communal and social organizations.

The curriculum for each speciality is drawn up by the Ministry of Higher and Specialized Secondary Education. The day courses preparing technicians for future employment include three distinct periods.

In the first period the student receives both general and technical education, acquires a knowledge of the natural sciences concerned, and learns the practical skills of a working trade. Many of the *technicums* have their own workshops where the students make instruments and simple machine tools.

After the introductory period of 2 to 3 years and the acquisition of a working trade, the students embark upon a year of productive work in industry. They are regularly employed and receive normal wages based on the actual work completed. During the second period academic instruction is continued in the evening or by correspondence, particularly in those subjects related to the students' employment.

In the third period, the students return to the college and are again eligible for the academic stipend. During this period, they take an examination in their specialization, continue their programme, outline their project, and finally complete and defend their diploma project.

The curriculum of any *technicum* course may be regarded as composed under three main headings: general education, technical subjects and special technical studies. The content of the first is maintained on a level equal to the general secondary schools, and in this section literature, mathematics, history, sciences, languages and physical education are included. A uniform level achievement is thus assured in secondary education, general or specialized, throughout the Soviet Union.

Likewise, the uniformity of composition of the general technical section is maintained over a wide area of technical activity and includes such fundamental subjects as technical drawing, mechanics and electrotechnics.

In the special technical cycle the subjects are those which are related to the speciality chosen. For example, the curriculum of the speciality 'boilers' includes the special subjects, working of metals, foundry practice and the basis of welding techniques.

The whole course comprises extensive laboratory and design office work, including two or three projects. The type of project is determined by the speciality of the student and involves the detailed drafting of construction mechanisms. The content of the projects of the final course varies between colleges but efforts are made to implement them as a practical realization of the experience gained by the student during the second period.

This diploma project is the culmination of the programme and its purpose is to improve the existing technical processes, organization and methods of the industries concerned by outlining more modern instrumentation, or better design of the machine parts. Many of the diploma projects undertaken by graduates of *technicums* have been adopted by the industries concerned.

In some branches the attendance curriculum is arranged on a seasonal basis, studying during the winter only and doing practical field-work in the summer. Similarly the students in the evening and correspondence courses pursue only the theoretical subjects of the course, the practical training being covered by their daily employment. It is a necessary condition that before termination of the *technicum* course and qualification, the student following the correspondence or the evening course must have had a year's working experience in employment appropriate to his speciality. Since there is no unemployment in the Soviet Union, this presents no difficulty.

United Kingdom

The schemes of technician training described below apply with only slight modifications to England, Wales, Scotland and Northern Ireland. There are three separate authorities all having some control over the status of technician; the Ministry of Education re-constituted in 1964 as the Department of Education and Science; the professional institutions, being chartered associations of professional engineers having statutory authority from the Privy Council for professional education of their members; and the City and Guilds of London

Institute, founded in 1878, which although originally concerned mainly with skilled worker qualifications, now has a series of technician qualifications, especially in mechanical and electrical engineering.

The technical college

Leaving school at the minimum age of 15, the intending technician enters a part time course at the local technical college known as the General Course in Engineering. Attendance is usually paid and is arranged to fit in accordance with his employment and working hours, i.e., with wages paid. The course lasts 2 years and is intended to be diagnostic and selective. At the end of a year, according to his performance, the student is either transferred to a City and Guilds technician course, permitted to continue into the second year of the course, or relegated to a skilled worker course.

Only the more academically minded who show unusual promise in mathematics are advised to follow the second option. All others are advised to follow the first option.

Following the first option, the young student attending only part-time will pass the first part of this qualification in 2 years, and pass the second part in 4 years. These CGLI qualifications have only recently been established but are already rendering a valuable service. After the second part it is possible to take supplementary subjects and gain a 'full technological certificate'. This level is approximately equivalent to that of an associate degree in the United States.

The national certificate system

If the student chooses the second option, he will take an examination at the end of the second year upon terminating the general course. The results of this examination determine his future course. The subjects of the examination are graded with 'pass' or 'credit', the latter being the higher. Two credits and one pass enable the student to enter a programme for the National Certificate. With three passes, he may enter the second year o the CG technicians' courses described above. Less than three passes places the student in the first year of the same course, or in a craft (skilled worker) course.

Those who gain entry to the National Certificate courses are joined by those who leave school at 16 with a General Certificate of Education in at least four subjects, including mathematics ad science. Together they commence a 4-year part-time (one day and one evening per week) course which leads to the Ordinary National Certificate after 2 years, and to the Higher National Certificate after 4 years. These courses are under the control of joint ccmmittees composed of representatives of the Department of Education and Science, the professional institutions concerned, and a representative of the technical colleges.

The Higher National Certificate at a technical level is slightly higher than a United States associate degree and approximates the qualification of *Ingenieur* of the Federal Republic of Germany though the breadth of study is smaller with little outside the minimum technical subjects necessary for the particular occupation.

Further courses called 'endorsement' subjects may be added in 1 or 2 subsequent years and may lead to full professional status as a chartered engineer which ranks with a university degree.

The National Certificate system has been in operation in the United Kingdom for over 40 years and the programme attracts a great many students. In 1962, 20, 134 candidates were awarded the ONC and 11. 049 the HNC. Its main weakness is the length of time required to qualify. No one can acquire an HNC in less than 6 years, i.e., before the age of 21 starting at the minimum school-leaving age of 15, and most will be somewhat older through late starting or 1 or 2 years' failure.

Various methods have therefore been sought to shorten the time including: full-time courses with the award names changed to Ordinary, and Higher, National Diploma; sandwich courses, alternating college study and works experience in approximately equal proportions; and entry at a higher standard. In the last case the student may enter upon leaving school at 18. Those having at least one subject pass in the GCE at advanced level may enter a full-time or sandwich course for the Higher National Diploma and gain this qualification in 2 years' full-time or in 3 years' 'sandwich' attendance.

There is a continuous gradation of qualifications from skilled worker to the higher technician and professional levels, and a continual re-orientation of individual students according to their proven abilities. Diagnosis is made as much upon the marks gained during the whole of the course as upon examinations at the end of it. Advice given by the college staff to the student is not always obligatory.

The student may reject it and make his own choice if he so wishes provided that the complies with the conditions necessary to pass to the next stage.

The description given has purposely avoided detail in order that the general pattern may be followed. There are in fact many other possibilities such as transfer from the final year of a craft (skilled worker) course to the second year of a technician course, or from the final of the CG technicians' course to a National Certificate course with exemption of 1 or 2 years.

With the better employers, day-release with wages paid is normally given in the engineering, building and many other industries. After the age of 18, attendance may have to be in the evenings, usually three periods per week of 2 or 21/2 hours.

Further education

The administrative section of the Department of Education and of the Local Education Authorities dealing with this form of education, whether full r part-time, is known as 'further education', and runs parallel, to some extent, with 'higher education', the term usually used to indicate the work of universities, including former colleges of advanced technology and teacher-training establishments.

The system for the training of technicians in the United States, an extension of the secondary-school system. It solves the problem outlined in the preface to this chapter of whether practice or college study should come first, providing these concurrently or in short alternations (sandwich courses). It requires much co-operation between education and industry with employers willing to pa-wages for day-release attendance. There is no statute compelling them to do so. although the provisions of the Industrial Training Act 1964 may reimburse employers for these costs.

United States of America

It is only in recent years that the public and, in particular, those engaged in education in the United States have become acutely conscious of the need for training at the technician level. The technical institute had in fact been a feature of the United States educational system for over a century though its functions were negligible and its work was almost unknown. A report published in 1931 could find only nine institutions in the United States of the type now qualifying as technical institutes. The characteristic feature of such institutions is a 2-year full-time course, terminal and occupational in character, gaining a specified diploma and often accompanied by an associate degree recognized by the State.

The engineers council for professional development

In 1944 the Engineers Council for Professional Development began a scheme of accrediation for technical institute curricula as it had done earlier for full, 4-year degree courses in colleges and universities. From time to time in the annual reports of that council and elsewhere, lists of these accredited institutes are published.

In addition the junior colleges movement in the United States, and in particular its counterpart, the community college, had been for several years setting up 2-year programmes preparing students for transfer to a 4-year college at the third year level, or for employment after graduation, these courses being known as 'vocational terminal programmes. Some of the latter programmes have been accredited by the ECPD and many others award the associate degree after recognition by the state. Some of the 4-year colleges and universities, in addition to their 4-year programmes as we.. In 1958 the total number of institutions offering such course of not less than 1 nor more than 3 years' duration was 757, of which 264 included technical studies. The enrollments were 206, 374, of which 76, 112 were in technical courses.

In 1961, 197 technical colleges had 36,186 full-time enrollments. Of these, only 32 colleges, 17,090 fill-time and 7.041 part-time students were accredited by the ECPD.

The level of such technical training, if the ECPD-accredited course is considered alone, falls somewhat below that of *Ingenieur* of the Federal Republic of Germany and comes between the United Kingdom levels of Ordinary and Higher National Certificates.

Comparison is difficult in he latter case since the United States course contains a wider range of subjects with slightly lower technical standard.

The standard of the remainder of the vocational terminal courses is subject to some state but no federal control and it is therefore difficult to make an exact appraisal of the value of na associate degree for the United States as a whole.

Entry to such course at age 18 requires the applicant to have a high school diploma, but subjects like mathematics and science are often recommended. Such a level is usually below the level of the year preparing the French *baccalaureate* or the United Kingdom General Certificate of Education at 'ordinary level, 4 subjects'.

The graduates of these courses are now, after some initial hesitation, sought after United States industry. A survey made between 1949 and 1961 by the Southern Technical Institute in the state of Georgia, covering 985 individuals, noted that the average commencing salary in 1961 was $400 per month rising to $751 after 12 years.

There are various substitutes for full-time attendance, e.g., pat-time, day and/or evening, and co-operative study. This last option is the United States counterpart of the United Kingdom sandwich system, i.e., alternate periods of college and works training.

The total number of graduates is approximately 12.000 of whom only 6.035 were ECPD-accredited. Compared with the number of 'first way' engineers, approximately 36,000 per year, this gives an inverse ratio of one in three. The scarcity of technicians has in fact been evident for some time and under Title VIII of the National Defense Act 1958, a vigorous attempt is being made to remedy the situation.

National defense (education) act 1958

This act was the culmination of the movement to extend and improve education in the United States. Only Title VIII dealing with area vocational education concerns technicians. It authorizes federal subsidy, dollar for dollar, to state funds to provide for (a) full time programmes for high school students in their last 2 or 3 years, tenth, eleventh, twelfth grade; (b) full-time follow-on programmes for high school graduates from 18 years upwards; and (c) extension courses for those in employment. The courses in the first group are virtually the same as those given in a secondary technical school but the curriculum offers a closer occupational basis than heretofore, whilst those in the second group cover technician training at the first level. It comes near in standard to the full technical institute level of work.

The two grades of technician in the United States are now commonly categorized as industrial technician and engineering technician. The latter is ECPD-accredited and the former may be the product of a technical school. THe definitions, however, are still not precise.

In recent years, recognition of technicians has become a little better organized with the foundation in 1962 of the Institute for the Certification of Technicians. This body was sponsored by the National Society of Professional Engineers but is now an independent organization. Its board of trustees consists of four professional engineers and four senior engineering technicians, the latter being the highest from of membership in the new institute. This institute does no teaching, and does not accredit courses, this being done by the ECPD. The sole purpose of the institute is to accredit technicians as individuals and to issue a membership card in their name denoting their status.

There are three levels of membership : junior technician, technician and senior technician and senior technician, with minimum requirements to be met through examinations with a view to raising the prestige status of the technician and clarifying the question of grade of qualification.

In addition to the 2-year full-time courses described above there are many part-time and evening courses. A few of these course but rarely do so. There is no clearly defined national qualification in the United States which corresponds to the United Kingdom Ordinary National Certificate or to the Tekniker of the Federal Republic of Germany, although every large town has evening courses. These courses are extension departments of a university and prepare students for acceptance by that university. They also award their own degree. For example, using the premises of the Massachusetts Institute of Technology, the Lowell Institute organizes a 2-year evening course in both mechanical and electrical subjects. Attendance is for six hours per week for 30 weeks per year. THe requirements for admission are similar to those for a United Kingdom Ordinary National Certificate.

Extension divisions of universities frequently organize part-time or short full-time courses of 20 to 30 hours' total attendance in specialized subjects. Pennsylvania State University offers this sort of course for operators of water, sewage and industrial waste systems at three succeeding levels-basic, intermediate and advanced-awarding a Pennsylvania State Continuing Education Certificate upon termination of such studies.

There are also a number of private institutions offering full-time technician training of a type particularly appropriate to immediate industrial needs. The entrance fees to such institutions are high by European standards, so they are subjected to considerable pressure to limit the duration of studies to the minimum required to meet the standard. This has led some of these colleges to give continuous curses. This system is known as the 'four quarter systems. Careful planning of class-room and laboratory work reduces waste time to a minimum and frequent small tests keep students aware of their rate of progress. A few such private institutions are accredited by the ECPD.

Compared with the carefully controlled technician qualifications of Europe, the United States situation appears disorganized at best but it is quantity rather than quality that is lacking. This failing is shared by every country in the survey.

The need for expansion of training with in the wide range of attainments covered by the word technician has now been acknowledged by a rapid succession of relevant legislation. The Area Redevelopment Act of 1961 encourages training for a skill as a means of reducing unemployment.'

The Manpower Development Act of 1963 extends the already wide training powers of the 1962 Act. By November 1963. 56,000 persons were enrolled in such training under 525 different occupational titles. The Higher Education Facilities Act of 1963 has made grants for construction of new buildings and facilities with 22 per cent of the grant being reserved for technical institutes and community colleges. The Vocational Education Act of 1963 expands the old Smith-Hughes and George Barden Acts and perpetuates the temporary provisions of Title VIII of the National Defense (Education) Act of 1958.

11 Financing Technical Education

The expenditure of technical reflects not only the progress achieved in the field but also the organisational structure. Prior to Independence, the expenditure of the Central Government on technical education was negligible, and the bulk of the finances required was provided by the States and this was meagre. The contribution of private agencies was also negligible. As the Centre's initiative in the development of technical education grew, the Central Government has provided funds in an increasing measure every year, not only for its own institutions but as aid to State Governments and private institutions. There was a corresponding increases. Today, finance for technical education as a whole are derived mainly from these three sources viz, the Central Governments, State Governments and private agencies.

The first great fillip came with the First Five - Year Plan. during that plan period the Centre provided about Rs. 163.3 m. for technical education. A much larger outlay, viz, Rs 400m. which is more than twice that in the First Plan was provided for the Second Plan. These amounts include both developmental and normal expenditure. So far as the States are concerned, the outlay during the

First Plan was of the order of Rs. 70.0m. and about Rs. 266.6m in the Second Plan, exclusive of the assistance received from the Centre.

Exact figures of the expenditure incurred by private agencies are not readily available, bit it is estimated that this sector has contributed on an average about Rs. 5.0m. i.e., Rs. 50,00,000, per year in the last three to four years.

The importance of technical education to the national plan is further underlined by the fact that a much larger outlay is being made in the Third Five-Year Plan. According to the present estimates, an amount of about Rs. 1450m. is proposed to be spent by the Central and State Governments on the expansion of technical education at all levels.

Rising costs and economy measures

The increasing outlay on technical education is not entirely due to the establishment of an increasing number of institutions and a similar quantitative expansion of the facilities. It is in art due to the fact that the cost of technical education is rising sharply. No reliable data are available regarding the cost of establishment of an engineering college or polytechnic prior to 1948, since few, if any, new institutions, were then established. Also, no standards of instructional facilities required for degree or diploma courses in various subjects were laid down. On the basis of the standards now laid down by th All-India council, an engineering college with an annual admission capacity of 120 students for Civil, Mechanical and Electrical engineering costs today over Rs. 4.5, for buildings and equipment alone. The cost of land and its development for the establishment of the college, providing essential services, hostels, staff quarters, etc. are all extra. The running expenses of the college are of the order of Rs. 0.8m per year; if the salary scales recommendered by the All-India Council are offered to the staff. Not more than 25 per cent of the running expenditure is met by the income from tuition fees. Similarly, the cost of polytechnics also has gone up and is of the order of Rs. 1.8 -2.0m for buildings and equipment and Rs. 300,000 per year for recurring expenditure. When courses in special fields as, for instance, Mining, Metallurgy, Chemical Engineering etc. are added to a college, the cost goes up further.

A major financial and organisational confronting planners therefore, is how to bring down the cost without sacrificing standards. The problem is twofold. The first involves a consideration of the *per capita* expenditure. If the *per capita* expenditure is brought down by making an institution work longer hours and train a larger number of students, a quantitative expansion of the facilities can be secured at less cost than otherwise. An attempt in this direction has already been made during the last four years and the training capacity of a number of institutions has been expanded in preference to new institutions being established for the additional number of students. The same principle is being extended to new programmes, a substantial part of the Third Plan targets are proposed to be reached through an expansion of the existing institutions.

The second aspect involves the development of an indigenous scientific instruments industry. According to the present estimates, at last 50 per cent of the equipment required by an engineering college and 30 per cent of the equipment required by a polytechnics have to be imported. The prices of imported equipment are rising steeply and in th last three years alone, the prices of many items have gone up by about 50 per cent on an average. Apart from foreign exchange difficulties, such a large increase in the prices can upset completely the targets of a plan. The institutions will be hard put to, to equip themselves full within the allotted funds. The solution to the problem lies in the development of an indigenous industry and by making the country self-sufficient in essential scientific equipment of quality and precision. The institutions should be encouraged to make in their own workshops as many items as possible of equipment required by them. An expert Committee of the All-India Council has gone into this question and suggested measures to secure economy in equipment for technical institutions.

There is also the question of buildings that account for 50 percent of the capital cost of a technical institution. Good laboratories, classrooms, drawing halls, library, workshop and other facilities are, no doubt, necessary. But, grand and expensive buildings constructed with an eye to architectural impressiveness are not synonymous with good institutions. The expenditure purely functional and economical designs as also by employing modern construction techniques. We need to revise out order of priority, to give the first place to staff, the second to equipment and only the last to buildings.

Foreign aid

No report on Technical Education in India would be

complete without a reference to Foreign Aid, that has played no small part in the recent developments in this field. The aid has been given by many countries generously and in a spirit of co-operation and has been readily accepted by India. It consists of scientific, and technical equipment, and library; the services of expert professors in various branches of technology; and facilities for the training of the teachers of out institutions abroad. These are the three essential things that we need for the establishment and development of institutions of advanced technological studies.

Foreign Aid first came under the Unesco programme. Since 1951 this aid has been extended every year for developing facilities for advanced studies and research at selected centres. Aid under other programmes, as, for instance, U.S. Agency For International Development, Colombo Plan etc., followed in increasing measure. Recently, under bilateral and other arrangements, very large assistance has been provided by certain countries in the establishment and development of entire technological institutions. Special mention must be made of the assistance provided by the U.S.S. R. for the Western Higher Technological Institute at Bombay;' by the Federal Republic of Germany for the Southern higher Technological & Technology at Delhi; and by the U.S.A. for the higher Technological Institute at Kanpur. It is the valuable aid of these countries that will accelerate the establishment and development of these important institutions.

The extent of Foreign Aid provided or promised so far, for technical education in India is as below:

(a) Number of experts: 245

(b) Equipment: Rs. 55.0 million

(c) Number of Fellowships for the training of teachers abroad : 607

In addition, at least about 200 teachers have been trained or are under training on fellowships offered by various countries under other programmes. This is exclusive of aid given by certain countries such as the USA, Canada, etc., for rupee-expenditure on certain projects of technical education.

Practical training

The practical work done by students of technical institutions is an integral part of their training in becoming engineers and an important pre-requisite to successful technical studies. It serves many purposes. It acquaints students in practice with the production of materials, their moulding and processing, as well as with the finished products in composition, structure and mode of action. In addition, it familiarises them with the testing of a finished workpiece and with the assembly of machines and apparatus, installation on the site, and control. In Civil Engineering, the training has to deal with actual construction methods and techniques, stability and strength of structures and various other aspects relevant to that field. This is also true of other engineering fields in which appropriate to each of them the training has to deal broadly with the processes and techniques, operations and controls, the functioning and capacity of machines, all geared to the attainment of a re-determined objective.

Three-fold objective

According to this, the practical training has to fulfil three tasks. First, to acquaint the student with the production or construction methods. The training, for which only a limited time is available, has to be systematic so that the trainee may become acquainted with a whole range of methods and thus gain wider experience. The trainee should also try to understand the knowledge in that field. The training of specialist skilled workers and the practical training of students of engineering, are quite different things. The purpose in training the former is to impart to them the manual skill that is required in their occupation and that is acquired by repeatedly practicing on the same workpiece. The training of an engineering student, on the other hand, is intended to show him how the same final shape of a workpiece can be produced by means of different methods in accordance with constructional requirements. The workers' training is intensive; the students' practical Organisationally and administratively, it should have an identity of its own in relation to the aims and objects of part-time courses and involve itself with industry.

These special wings should work in close collaboration with industrial concerns and other organisations which are served by them. The collaboration should not be a one-way traffic. Industry should not only advice the institutions on the types of courses to be conducted for the benefit of the workers and similar aspects, but should participate actively in the working of the institutions. It should be an important part of the participation that industry provides the services of its experts as part-time teachers at the institutions.

Industry should encourage its promising workers to join the courses and offer them suitable incentives for the purpose in the form of part-day release form work, tuition fees etc. Professional advancement of the workers should follow as a recognition of the successful completion of the courses.

It is also necessary to bring the professional societies into this picture. The societies should advise the institutions on the standards of courses, and suitable arrangements should be developed whereby candidates completing the prescribed courses satisfactorily are considered as having fulfilled the requirements for the corporate membership of the societies and are thus recognised as professional engineers. To this end, the examinations may be held jointly by the institutions and professional societies or, alternately, the examinations held by the institutions are recognised by the societies after due assessment.

The institutions should offer a wide range of courses to meet the requirements of different groups of workers. some may be short courses to improve the operational efficiency of workers in their own fields. Some may be to prepare the workers for the state board diploma examinations and others to prepare them for the membership of professional societies. The question of conducting at the institutions university degree or equivalent courses on a part-time basis should also be seriously considered.

It is important that the training at the institutions is not narrowly professional but broad-based, educationally., This will not only advance the technical efficiency of the workers, but will raise their general educational level. The worker of today is the executive of tomorrow. He should be equipped for his new responsibilities through an educational process specially designed for the purpose. The institutions should, therefore, adopt a comprehensive and integrated approach to the problem, keeping in view at all stages the full social implications of technological progress.

Technology and The Man

"If the humanities cannot be of service to man during his busiest and most critical hours, then assuredly they are merely a frill for the home-spun of life. The Romans understood by the word *Humanities* the practical, daily use of great literature, art and philosophy by those men who had learned the moral, intellectual and imaginative power which habitual association with the nest minds of civilization confers. The function of the course, then, is to enable students to think somewhat as the masters have thought about divine, human and eternal nature, and to enable them to feel to some extent the wonder, and awe, the spiritual elevation and power that the masters have felt when their insight into the forces of life has compelled them to produce artistic imitations or philosophic or scientific analyses so that lesser men might also penetrate the abstractions of the world".

Grand words-but the truth assumes a more practical from when a broad view is taken of the potential professional character of engineering as well as of the values that are inherent in the Humanities and Social Sciences. In the education of the professional engineer, the function of the Humanities and Social Sciences is not limited to the improvement of communication skills and the emergence of amiable employees. Nor is the primary function to provide a history of the arts, a convenient catalogue of factual information which is quickly consulted and used in conservation with cultured business associates. It is comparatively unimportant whether students know that the theory of flux preceded Plato's ideal of unvarying truth or that Bach was celebrated for polyphonic harmony and 20 children. The engineer is a social consequences. Whether he is aware of it or not, he is instrumental in the creation of a new society and a new economic order, as well as a new physical environment. One result of his professional accomplishments is that he is called upon to accept an increasingly responsible role as leader of his community. To discharge his growing responsibilities the engineer needs both professional competence, a sure understanding of himself and of the world in which he lives. He needs 'depth, flexibility and a capacity for growth in directions in which we ourselves can today only dimly visualise'. The business of an engineering education is to provide him with a foundation upon which he may build a career of genuinely professional stature.

With this in view, the Humanities and Social Sciences can for us take their appropriate place as an integral part of total education. They do not stand apart from the rest of the curriculum; they support the scientific-technical training, and are in turn supported by it. They contribute to professional competence not merely in the narrowly vocational sense but in the broad sense of enabling the engineer to see his own activities in their human and social contexts. Even beyond this broad concept of professional development, the Humanities and Social Sciences represent for the engineer, as for all men, the heart of an inherited experience.

For well over 20 years, all advanced countries have given much attention to the crucial problem of how to develop and maintain an effective programme of humanistic-social studies in technological education. In the U.S.A. alone nearly 80 universities and technical institutions are actively engaged in this work and the American Society for Engineering Education has done much to promote an educational philosophy that is acceptable to the engineering and liberal arts faculties. The large volume of literature that has emerged on the subject bears ample testimony to the importance of the problems.

Both at out universities and technical institutions in general, not much effort has been made to integrate humanistic- social studies into technological courses and to realise the full value of the contributions that the liberal arts can make to the training of engineers. The curriculum of many institutions are conspicuous for the absence of any reference to the humanities; in some, only a passing reference has been made but the subjects suggested viz. English Composition and Report Writing are intended only to improve the communication skill of the students. At the Higher Technological Institutes, however, a purposeful attempt is being made to profit by the valuable experience of other countries in this respect. A full-fledged Department of Humanities and Social Sciences has been established at the Indian Institute of Technology, Kharagpur, whose objectives are defined as below:

> "In order to broaden the student's outlook beyond the limits of his immediate academic and professional interest, all undergraduate courses include a certain amount of non-technical, cultural and social studies which are grouped under the general designation of the Humanities".

The recommendations of the Hammond Report to the American Society for Engineering Education are of particular value to our universities. The goals of what that report called the "humanistic-social stem" were stated, not in terms of subject-matter, but in terms of competences which the Humanities and Social Sciences could help the student acquire:

(a) An understanding of the evolution of the social organisation within which we live and of the influence of science and engineering on its development.

(b) The ability to recognise and make a critical analysis of a problem involving social and economic elements, to arrive at an intelligent opinion about it, and to read with discrimination and purpose towards these ends.

(c) The ability to organise thoughts logically and to express them lucidly and convincingly in oral and written English.

(d) An acquaintance with some of the great masterpieces of literature and an understanding of their setting in and influence on civilization.

(e) The development of moral, ethical, and social concepts essential to satisfying personal philosophy, to a career consistent with the public welfare and to a sound professional attitude.

(f) The attainment of an interest and pleasure in these pursuits and thus of an inspiration to continued study.

The time has now come for Indian universities to address themselves to this problem of humanistic social studies and to reconstruct their technological curriculum along more enduring and useful lines.

12 Instructional Technology

Introduction

Technology is a force of significance in most aspects of modern civilization and it is no less significant in the field of education. Instructional technology does not simply mean machines in the classroom, however, it means much more than that.

Educational media are crucial to the individual learner because they represent an alternative means of his accessing relevant information in the absence of a traditional teacher/lecturer. In the general sense, educational media include texts, workbooks, programmed books and other print materials; tapes, records and other audio materials: filmstrips, motion pictures, study prints and other photographic materials; games, realia, apparatus and a number of other manipulative materials; charts, signs maps, and other graphic materials; dioramas, bulletin boards, felt boards and other displays; as well as a variety of other cue-organizing resources which serve as the carriers of messages. many of these media-based messages are accessed by the individual learner in his classroom, others are obtained in a school resource center, and still others must be obtained from remote locations.

Television, dial access systems, shared-time computers, and the telephone are all techniques for accessing remote educational material.

It is *not* necessary to have sophisticated technology in order to individualize learning and many "audio-visual" resources currently in use are quite well suited to this application.

Finally, recognizing that the term technology refers as much to a process as to a set of hardware and media alternatives, it is useful to examine how the process of technology may alter the man-machine relationship in the days and years to come. Then, through the analysis of school management needs, evaluative research needs, and instructional needs it should be possible to reallocate those functions which technology can appropriately perform, freeing professional educators to provide more personalized attention to individual students. A model of a System for Individualized Instruction Management shows how this might work.

Man, ritual, the establishment and instructional technology

Appointment of a national Commission on instructional Technology under the Public Broadcasting Act points up the need for broad participation in defining agreeable boundaries of the field, locating the problem within its human, social, and institutional contexts, and considering priorities of emphasis and action.

The Commission's assignment is complicated by a posture of pessimism in a new power structure of instructional technology, or "learning systems," particularly among these involved in adapting computers to instruction. This posture appears to be based on the partial truth that instructional technological devices have failed to live up to overstated performance promises when adopted by the schools. Consequently, all technological innovation, including those in various stages of R.&D., are viewed as vulnerable to the dreadful disclosure of fraud when submitted to the pragmatic test of trial and adoption in actual instructional situations. The fact that many schools and colleges are virtually without funds intensifies the new pessimism toward instructional technology.

Factors underlying pessimism

Underlying this pessimism or defeatism are several identifiable factors which lie deep in the educational system as sources of many problems of instruction. The salience of these factors is well known to those who have (a) participated directly in technological innovation in public school systems, colleges, and mass military training; (b) done both contextual and evaluation research on what hitherto have been known as "new media in education"; and (c) tried to develop viable theories dealing with the "new media in instruction."

1. An over expectation of effects from any given gadget or process, simple or complex, adapted to instruction from some other area, such as entertainment and automated industrial processes and commercial transactions.

2. "Measurement of effects" of the "new media" by instruments and techniques which are non-metric in the mathematical sense of measurement and insensitive to dimensions of

human response that may be of much greater importance than the "behavioural objectives" they are designed to "measure."

3. A "Scientific" outlook among learning theorists, instructional systems analysts and designers, programmed instruction developers, etc., which (a) ignores the importance and operation of intuition in classroom interaction, and (b) prescribes narrow behavioural objectives and their criterial "measures."

4. An inertial property of educational and adjunct institutions which makes them resistant to change, slow to innovate, and methodological non-adaptive when innovation is tried.

5. An irrelevance of much of learning theory of classroom teaching situations as they exist in reality, rather than in psychology laboratories.

6. A curriculum which is frequently misphased, overintellectualized, and irrelevant to the individual needs and social milieu of large umbers of students, and consequently operative at best among bright and/or docile students responsive to pressures for compliance from both parents and teachers.

7. An overextended period of compulsory or socially prescribed education which induces boredom and maintains the status quo in a seller's market in formal education, and an underdeveloped program of continuing education which is particularly receptive and adaptive to instructional technology.

It seems the better part of valor in the present state

of things to adopt a moderate view of the scope of instructional technology. Otherwise, we will become involved in a range of concerns from team teaching to underground, windowless schools.

Essentially, instructional technology in its modern usage, involves the *management* of ideas, procedures, money, machines, and people in the instructional process. As such, it involves:

1. A physical device(s) which mediates information transmission.
2. A system of instruction of which this device(s) is one of several components; and
3. A range of mediating options involving progression in (a) requirements for physical alternation of the "classroom"; (b) remoteness in time and space between the tutor-planner and the student; (c) sophistication of design of programmed information exchange between "tutor" and student; (d) complexity and cost of hardware; (e) level of technical skills required for equipment construction, installation, "de-bugging," operation, and maintenance; (f) independence from classroom teacher control or continuous monitoring in the operation of th device centered "teaching"; (g) additional manpower required by way of paraprofessional personnel for use of the instructional technology; and (h) role changes and new skills required of "classroom" teachers in (1) management of the technology, and (2) other and/or new non-structured, non-mediated teaching activities essential to personality development, humanistic growth, and cultivation of values, all of which lie

outside the present and foreseeable potential of instructional technology as herein considered.

While the progression in technological devices indicated above is not deliberately sequenced in order of increasing administrator and teacher resistance to technological innovations in education, such a heuristic resistance sequence is implicit.

Classroom teacher ritual

The current and historical role of the classroom teacher is highly ritualized. Any major change in ritual is likely to be resisted as an invasion of the sanctuary by the barbarians.

Ritualization in teaching is flexible enough to permit idiosyncrasies of personal style, arrangement of the daily schedule, police methods, pacing, etc., *but major characteristics of ritual tend to be invariant.*

Two of these invariants are (I) teacher control of the teaching - testing - grading - reward - punishment processes, and (2) face-to-face interaction with students. These two variants in rituals of teaching are likely to be important determinants in the trial and adoption of technological innovation and in its effectiveness in either event at the classroom level.

Any *sudden or substantial reduction of* dominance status and/or domain of activities of the classroom teacher, any major change in the interpersonal teacher-student communication situation, or any systematic attempt to scientize and rationalize the intuitively determined interaction patterns of the teacher is likely to elicit at least some teacher hostility and resistance.

The attitude of the classroom teacher toward any instructional innovation-technological or otherwise-is of paramount importance. While trial or adoption of innovation may be formalized at the federal, state, or community levels of control, it is in the individual school and individual classroom that the transaction occurs functionally.

Indeed, it may be that the more or less generally accepted theory of instructional innovation as (a) originating from the outside and (b) proceeding from the top down in the hierarchical structure, carriers within it the seeds of its own failures or imperfections by omitting participation of classroom teachers in adaption and adoption decisions at the local policy making and implementation level.

Some remarkable research findings with direct bearing on the effect of teacher attitudes on student behavior are currently being spelled out by Robert Rosenthal and his associates using the concept of communication of expectancy.

In studies of the introduction or programmed instruction in Denver, Colorado, it was reported that students performed better under teachers favorable to programmed instruction *even when the sole function of the teacher was to maintain order.* Put another way, better results were obtained from students under programmed instruction when the expectancy of teachers was in a favorable direction, and this expectancyeffect occurred independently of the participational activity role of the teachers in the instructional process.

Apparently, human beings are highly sensitive

to both intended and unintended expectancy curing behavior of other human beings in dominant roles. Rosenthal reports that in an experiment on perception of people through photographs, subjects were asked to rate the experimenters on the "honesty" variable. This variable could be operative only after the experiment, and could occur in tabulating and summing the results. Errors in tabulation could be random or in the direction of confirming the hypothesis held by the experimenter, and tabulation and computational errors could be large or small.

Both tabulation an computational errors occurred. Among those who erred in th direction of the expectancy of their hypotheses, tabulation errors were larger. Mean ratings on an honesty scale by the experimental subjects were significantly lower for those experimenters who made errors in the direction of their hypothesis, i.e, experimenter expectancy. This suggests that subjects in the experiment were able to detect some cues in the behavior of experimenters which predicted beyond chance the subsequent errors in experimental data processing.

This apparent sensitivity of subjects to unitentional and perhaps non-formally coded cues to expectancy of results manifested by authority figures in an authority-structured social situation can be related to teacher influence on student performance in the direction of their expectancy hypothesis in the Denver trials of programmed instruction-especially when monitoring teachers exercised only the police function of preserving order in the classroom.

Even more remarkable results of teacher expectance on student development of competencies are reported by Robert Rosenthal and Lenore Jacobson in their recent books *Pygmalion in the classroom*. Teachers in a San Fransisco Bay Area school were told that about 20 percent of the students in each class included in the experiment had been identified through extensive testing as having unusual potential for intellectual gains. No such extensive testing had been done. The name of the 20 percent identified as having this unusual potential were selected randomly.

In this experiment no special programs, tutoring activities, or enrichment activities were involved. The only new element was that of favorable teacher expectation-teacher attitude toward the "unusual" pupils-and presumably consequent verbal and non-verbal expression by the teachers of this attitude toward these students.

To oversimplify interesting results, "unusual" students made significantly greater gains in IQ than the non-unusuals. The implication of these findings are difficult to overestimate. They suggest that (a) teacher expectancy, often operating at the unintentional level, is a variable of major importance in the instructional and developmental processes; and (b) students are highly sensitive and responsive to teacher expectancy along previously unsuspected dimensions of perception and growth.

It is reasonable to assume teacher expectance operates negatively as well as positively, as suggested by the Denver findings. That is, negative teacher exportancy may have a depressing, or leveling, or inhibiting, or hostility-arousing effect on student development. Yet, as far as I know, teacher selection and certification procedures do not ordinarily include the criterion of the true believe in the "unusual" growth potential of students.

It may be hypothesized that all innovators and agents of change tend to be what Eric Hoffer calls "true believers," oriented toward toward a better future of mankind, and improvement of the human condition of everyone; and that one of the most important aspects of instructional technology is the inherent expectancy of educational improvement shared by its advocates. The corollary is that instructional technology fail or disappoints when its implementation falls into the hands of skeptics and infidels whose habituated classroom rituals have attained doctrinal significance, and consequently whose expectancy of ritualistic change is negative.

Crystallization of the argument

To crystallize the argument, it should be borne in mind that:

1. Many of the troublesome problems of instructional technology are essentially further manifestations of the troublesome problems and properties of instruction in the American educational system.

2. The fashionable attitude of pessimism and "pooh-pooh" toward instructional technology is particularly evident among an elite of the superior Educational Establishment for whom the world of instructional technology originated last year or the year before and consist largely of promised by undelivered computer regulation of the process of individualized, multi-tracked

instructional programs, task assignments, and performance monitoring.

3. At least some, if not many of the significant variables of in-school growth and development of students lie beyond the cognizance of learning theory, and the consequences of these variables escape the narrowly prescribed "first order," behaviorally operationalized objectives of instruction and their criterial "measures".
4. The process of innovation has been studied on the normative rather than the explanatory, i.e., theoretical, level and consequently the literature on innovation provides few cues for acceleration and adoption of desirable changes in the system of instruction.
5. The classroom teacher is by training and institutional control a prisoner of the orthodox Ritualization of the educational system, negatively disposed to automation, and perhaps less effective as a gatekeeper than as a positive or negative expectancy reflector.

It follows that substantial, difficult, and not-clearly defined changes must be made in the educational system both for its own effective survival and in order to accelerate the rate of development, adoption, and optimum use of instructional technology, assuming that instructional technology can be justified in the first place.

Justification of instructional technology

Instructional technology is more justified by its own logic than by empirical studies of its effectiveness in facilitating "learning." Empirical studies often ignore critical variables, and typically "measure" only those results which are easiest to operationalize within the state of the art of criterial specification and educational testing. The notion of "unobtrusive measures" has scarcely penetrated educational research and at least some of the vigorously promoted techniques of multivariate analysis are too often used as substitutes for thinking. This is not to say that empirical research has no place in uncovering important relationships or evaluating procedures and progress in instruction, but only that too often it is overburdened by techniques and designed with impoverished insight and imagination.

The development, use, and improvement of instructional technology, and defined in this article, is justified in general by the fact that American schools operate as a formative institution of a highly technological society and should therefore incorporate, as appropriate, this characteristic of the larger society as well as other idealized values. In a sense, this principle of justification is aesthetic and can rest at that without decisive challenge.

However, since aesthetics generates much subjectivity and little objectivity, stimulates lofty dialogue at the philosophical level and restless, insistent controversy in relation to specific events, it is desirable to get down to tangible criteria in justifying instructional technology.

It may be said reflectively that instructional technology is justified if and when it:

(a) makes available a mode or multimodes of representation on any of several levels of relatively without constrains of geography of of real time, and hitherto not available for introduction.

(b) provides a model of behavior otherwise unavailable, in scarce supply, or lacking authenticity or correctness of definition, and preferably when it provides opportunity for the student to compare his imitate behavior with that of the model.

(c) sequences and, within reasonable limits and without undue restraints, manages stimulus inputs and response outputs on a desirable individualized and structured basis otherwise difficult or impossible to achieve:

(d) stores, retrieves, and rapidly processes a large amount of important and useful information not otherwise readily available, or, if available, too time-consuming to process manually;

(e) involves desirable latent functions of a critical nature in the instructional process or system which, because they are not immediately related to improved and "measured" student progress, may escape proper assessment or even official observation.

None of these five criteria in necessarily independent of the other four. All can be combined in instructional systems involving simple or complex hardware, or electronic components. Also, it goes without saying that this brief list of criteria is not intended to be either definitive or exhaustive.

Minimizing contingencies of instructional technology

For what it is worth, it may be said reflectively, and with some empirical evidence, that the effectiveness of instructional technology will be less than optimum if and when it:

(a) incorporates the format of other modes of instruction known to be relatively inefficient and ineffecitve instructionally, i.e., when McLuhan's "rearview mirror" effect occurs;

(b) fails to challenge or slows down the natural pace of progression of students and thus induce student boredom and/or resentment:

(c) rapidly reaches a point of diminishing returns and thus becomes monotonous and unrewarding;

(d) severely and continuously reduces the social process of education, i.e., face-to-face interpersonal interactions, group participation, etc.;

(e) requires logistical support beyond the capacity of the system to provide in proper time-phase and matching characteristics, and without heavy encumbrance of hardware, additional personnel, or hard-to-find dollars.

13 Technological Changes and Education

The work of the school master was once comparatively simple, but like his rural employers he lacked scientific knowledge and equipment. A rapidly growing technology, however, has produced striking changes both in agricultural and in education. Before discussing what are sometimes referred to as the new medical of instruction, it may be profitable to examine and available the old and the current as the means that teachers now have at their disposal for controlling and managing the environment in order to promote learning. The possibilities of combining all available media in a modern educational technology can then be considered.

Traditional media

We would not expect any one medium to take the place of all the others, but it is possible that each has certain functions that it can perform most effectively and to the advantage of all concerned. The traditional media are, of course, famillar enough, but it is interesting to consider them from a comparative point of view.

The spoken word

The earliest medium of instruction was the spoken

word. In homes, churches, and armies, on farms, and in business and industry, as well as in the schools, the older people have told the younger what was expected of them/ Telling was formalized educationally in the lecture. The medieval scholastics read to the assembled students in the days when there were no printed books and few manuscripts. Now with unlimited textual material professors still lecture, and teachers spend most of the class time in talking. Some of this talk is informative; some, no doubt therapeutic for the teacher, serving to relieve his feelings. No one knows how much of this talk goes unheeded, or how much in understood. Probably every teacher at one time or another has experienced a feeling of futility like the one who concluded a careful exposition by saying. "Now that is clear, whether you understand it or not." Some of the teacher's talk is corrective, providing feedback on pupil responses. Whether this is negative or positive and rewarding, as Skinner has said, as a mere reinforcing mechanism the teacher is out of date.

Children like teachers who are able to "explain things." but it is difficult to do this to the satisfaction of all in a class made of pupils of widely differing abilities. A tutor has the advantage, for he can address himself to the responses of one individual, give specific directions, receive and supply feed-back, reduce the number of trials, and so speed up and enrich learning. But even here, no one knows how well these tasks are performed. Demonstrations usually need a vocal accompaniment, and certainly there is no good reason to dispense with the competent discussion leader. On the other hand, pupils in the self-contained classroom may get a little tired of the same voice all day long, referred to by those who are opposed to the developing technology as "the living voice of the teacher." and sometimes as "the voice of the living teacher". While the spoken word will necessarily be an important medium of institution many teachers are glad for an occasional respite during which they can turn the responsibility over to some other medium.

The written word

Already the use of handwriting for instructional purposes has largely disappeared. Illuminated manuscript are museum pieces, and the teacher no longer has to set the model for the writing lesson. About all that is left is to present outlines, directions, regulations, and the like, on the chalkboard. Even in teacher-pupil planning, one of the pupil is usually designated as the recorder. Sometimes teachers "correct" the errors in written work. This provides a feedback, though delayed, and offers an excellent opportunity for individual instruction, although there is usually insufficient time to take advantage of it.

Familiar technological advances

What can teachers do to promote learning besides talk and write? A number of inventions, now largely taken for granted have already found their way into the pattern of conventional instruction.

Movable type-the printed word

The invention of printing from movable type in the fifteenth century equals the invention of the whool and of the steam and internal-combustion engines in the magnitude of the resultant social change. The profusion of printed materials has virtually outlawed illiteracy, and has provided an embarrassment of riches foe education, and at the same time presented a number of difficulties that have not yet been fully resolved. Textbooks have poured from the presses, but experts differ on the best ways to use them. Teachers read them to their classes, ask questions on them, refer students to them, follow them, reject them, select from them, and combine them in course outlines on mimeographed sheets.

Trade books, fiction or other, are produced, many in textbook format, and are studied at the rate of a few pages a day, assigned for outside reading, placed on open shelves, and sometimes locked in the school library because pupils have been negligent in returning them. In paperback editors they are available at drugstores and supermarkets. Workbooks are used for seat work and homework, and are rejected entirely. School libraries function as storage space, but nowadays more often as resource centers for encyclopedias, magazines, journals, newspapers, pamphlets, and public documents to supplement instruction. Granting that different subjects and different parts of the same subject may call for different proportions of oral and printed instruction, it is nevertheless time for a careful review of the teacher's role in relation to that of the librarian. Ten million elementary and 150.000 secondary school pupils attend schools that have no central library. The average amount spent per pupil on library books come to about half the average cost of one book. In some school systems new books are unavailable until late in the term because they have to be stamped and catalogued, while in others the necessary work is done more expeditiously by clerks in the central office before the books are sent out to the schools, thus freeing the school librarian for his properduties.

Those who fear that television or teaching machines will take the place of reading should be assured that the book is here to stay. It is noteworthy that information about, the new media is found in printed form, not on screen or programme, though the latter may be called in for an assist now and then. More information can be provided more conveniently in book or pamphlet form than in any other. Although after leaving school, people may be taught or trained in specific content by means of the new media, these will not always be available, and so earlier practice should have the learner make frequent and profitable use of printed material. Indeed this is just what has happened in some school experimental situations. Particularly after some screen presentation or discussion, pupils have flocked to the library for materials that have been referred to.

One of the chief advantages of the book over oral instruction is that the pupil can go at his own rate, whereas in oral instruction, the teachers sets the pace, which may be about right for the average, but it likely to be too slow or too fast for others. An instructional materials center, of which the library is a part, is in the blueprints of many new schools.

Typewriter and offset processes

After nearly two centuries of experimentation, the

type-writer came into common use and subsequently the mimeograph, ditto machine, and various offset processes. These made it possible, at relatively low cost, to prepare print-like copies of course and lecture outlines and other data, to say nothing of examinations.

It is doubtful that as much use is made of these materials as should be. Lectures often report data collected with great effort and leave the student to get as much in his notes as possible for future reference. Slides and filmstrips, to be discussed later, may be used to present such data, but in practice often the fateful, "Next slide please", comes so quickly that the listeners have insufficient time to comprehend what is on the screen, to say nothing of making a record of it. As is often done, a lecture can present some materials in mimeographed from for later study. Like the screen, duplicated material enables all those in the room to loot at the same things at the same time, but only the latter permits later review.

Camera-The picture

Since comenius in the seventeenth century published the first school picturebook, illustrations have played an increasingly important part in instruction. From the crude drawings of *Orbus picture and the New England Primier* and the woodcuts of some early college textbooks we have come a long way to the photograph in black and white and in colour that we find in today's textbooks. Some do little more than lend attractiveness and charm. Others provide what early educational psychologists referred to as sense training and, later object teaching. The picture is not only a remarkably able substitute for realities beyond the reach of the school child it is also a means to aid him in perceiving significant cues so that discriminations are more precise and concept more quickly and accurately formed.

Projector-The screen

The "magic lantern," metamorphosed into the projector with slides and film strips, and then the overhead and opaque projectors, provided a most important extension in the use of the photograph, namely group observation and also convenience in storing, Now, instead of handing pictures around to the class or displaying them at the front where those at the back and sides of the room cannot see them, the teacher can flash them on the screen and all may clearly observe and discuss the same item at the same time. It is often easier to talk about something then to demonstrate it though the latter may be more effective. Many kinds of visual materials besides those mentioned-flannel boards, magnetic chalk boards, mape, globes, charts, graphs, models, mock-ups, cut-aways, exhibits, and simulators-can be used advantageously do for demonstration for different purposes.

The motion picture camera added a valuable through sometimes unnecessary component. Motion is of little value in presenting a picture of a mountain, a leaf, a geological formation or a painting, for example,. But to illustrate a storm, a lava flow, a machine, a motor skill, or any process in which movement is the significant stimulus, a still picture is of course, far less satisfactory. Slow motion or time expansion and time lapse or time compression, like magnification, reveal what cannot be seen otherwise. And the loop film can provide repetition of a model performance for imitation. It is hardly necessary to point out that projection can be of grant instructional value in narrowing the response to the significant aspects of the situation and in providing feedback from the pupil's own imperfect efforts, particularly in the motor skills.

Since most films are relatively short, they tend to be used as an adjust the supplement instruction. Probably as a consequence of the influence of educational television, whole courses, especially in science, supplemented by textbooks and workbooks, have been developed using 160 or so thirty-minute films. Such long series, like television programmes, provide skillful instruction, particularly demonstrations and explanations. Estimates suggest that school-owned films are most economical for programming a lesson series provided at least six schools use the set. If fewer, it is cheaper to rent. Thirty or forty schools are a better minimum for television. For closed circuit TV for fewer than four student sections, costs are higher than conventional instruction, but it has an advantages for 150 to 270 students.

Phonograph-The recording

The invention of the phonograph in the latter part of the nineteenth century did for sound what printing did for words and the camera for illustrations. It made possible their reproduction, wide diffusion, and convenient storage. First Edison's tinfoil, later his wax cylinder, then the disc and finally, in 1945, tape were used. For individual listening either separate listening booths or earphones are needed. Recordings have come into common educational use to bring the world's great music and drama into the schoolrooms. They provide feedback for training in speech an6 pronunciation of foreign languages. Connected with slides and filmstrips, they furnish the accompanying explanation of pictures, diagrams, or cartoons, or the directions for mechanical processes. In view of the increasing number of such processes, industrial concerns are finding this method very effective in trade training. It can be used to advantages in schools, particularly for teaching skills in ships, business, home economics, and arts and crafts courses, freezing the teacher to plan, supervise, and encourage, and so to bring the pupils to a higher level of performance.

The sound treak, added to the motion picture film in 1935, has resulted in a rich variety of products of high instructional value although some are apparently constructed with a view to making an appeal to such a wide range of interest and intelligence, that for many their value is questionable. At present, the projectors are still hard to transport, the may be in use in another part of the building, or out of order, so they have probably not been so widely used as they should be.

Audio-visual materials

If there is uncertainty about the role of the book, there us still more uncertainty about the role film and tape in education. Are they a means of instruction or merely aids or adjuncts to instruction? Basically, they are amplifiers which extend the range of the human voice, the eye, and car; or putting in another way, they bring distant sights and sounds into the schoolroom to individuals or any sized group a room will hold. As such, they are or can be a means of instruction just as a textbook is. But books are taken for granted whereas unfortunately audio-visual; materials are often introduced or not, largely at the whim of the teacher.

It would be interesting to speculate as to what would have been the result if film projection had been invented in the fifteenth century and the printing press in the nineteenth. The book would have had a race to overtake the picture and the spoken word. As a matter of fact, this is virtually what has happened where the battle for literacy is being waged, where there are no roads through swamp and jungle and the culture has jumped from the footpath to the airplane, skipping the oxcart, the horse and buggy, and the automobile. In such places, film flown in by air are presented in the native language which dew can read. Perhaps the audio-visual materials should precede the book even through they were invented later. It is possible that we do not make the sufficient use of the inventions we already have, nor make the equipment sufficiently accessible. Teachers should not have to run a film projector delivery service or repair shop. Technicians and others could well keep audio-visual materials in good condition and make them as available as the books in the library, and in many places they do.

There is probably little the matter with audio-visual programmes that a few more dollars and a little ingenuity could not cure. But as things now stand there is considerable dissatisfaction with the situation. A number of surveys and recommendations have noted the following needs. Better financial support. The $ 1.50 found to be the average amount spent per unit of average daily attendance was considered less than half what it should be.

More nearly adequate supply of materials

Development of standard cataloging and library procedures.

Increased assistance in curriculum planning and classroom use.

Statistical records and evaluations of audio-visual operations

additional housing space and light control facilities

Varying standards for allocations of equipment and floor space in districts differing in population density

Varying loan periods for different kinds of materials

More research on audio-visual education

strengthening of teacher education in new media utilization

In colleges, although most of the points would apply to the schools as well, resistance to the use of audio-visual materials was attributed to:

Faculty and administration ineria

Unavailability of films, equipment, or operators when needed

Lack of equipped classrooms or other viewing areas

Problems of obtaining the right material when needed

lack of budget to provide decentralization of certain materials and equipment

Unavailability of appropriate materials

Lack of information about sources

Limited time of instructors for locating of designing appropriate materials

Lack of technical assistance for preparation of materials

As previously stated, an instructional materials center is the solution many schools are trying.

New technological advances

A primitive technology early introduced the book for the use of the individual and, later audio-visual equipment for the group. Now, via cable and the airwaves, the possibilities of instruction are extended to individuals and groups in different parts of a building and even to different buildings and different localities. And programmed lessons make possible much greater precision and effectiveness in certain kinds of instruction.

Telephone-The Language Laboratory

The transmission of sound, direct or recorded, by wire and cable made possible by Bell's invention of the telephone in 1876 coupled with more recent electronic devices, opened the way for the language laboratory. Foreign languages, particularly Latin, Greek, and Hebrew, had been taught in America from the earliest days of secondary and higher educations. Since on one was expected to speak these languages, phonetics, grammer, composition, reading and literature were taught. When modern languages were introduced, traditional grammatical methods were followed with translation the objective. The ability to speak and understand the spoken languages was rarely sought and still more rarely attained. During World War I it was unpatriotic to know the language of the enemy, native German teachers were suspect and American teaches of German found themselves without students, while the teaching of French became as popular as the limited number of French teachers permitted. Sanity gradually returned, and during World War II the importance of modern language study was recognied, particularly for the forces that would occupy foreign territory. But for this purpose, translation was not so important as the ability to use the oral language. Relatively few foreign language teachers could do this and there was no time for the grammetical methods they knew.

Meanwhile the linguists had been studying the structure of language and the native language sounds-which, however, could not be taught satisfactorily by the usual class methods. The country was scoured for native speakers who drilled small groups on the language, sounds and expressions. Sometimes having the soldier students repeat words and stock sentences individually, a time-consuming method, or in union, which made individual correction difficult. A few language lessons based on the linguistic studies were recorded for the Army Area and Language programme. On these records, a native speaker would say a key sentence, then there would be a pause to give time for the student to repeat it. later developments produced the language laboratory on the principle of the juke box, with the recording of the native speaker centrally stored and the appropriate lessons transmitted through earphones. Teachers and those concerned with making programmes observe and help the students and correct and improve the programmes.

So obvious were the advantages of such a procedure that by 1962, according to a U.S. Office of Education survey, approximately 2500 secondary schools and over 700 colleges and universities were equipped with some kind of language laboratory. The advantage comes, however, not in recording old-fashioned grammer lessons, nor in using recordings as a mere adjunct to regular teaching. The language laboratory makes its greatest contribution when it is used as an integral part of a programme in which instruction in hearing and speaking forms the basis of sequential, cumulative, and carefully recycled development of language skill, each small step building directly on the preceding steps.

Materials and activities thus classify into three basic categories:

1. listening only, for aural comprehension and reading readiness;
2. repeating or "echoing", for improving pronunciation and unconsciously memorizing; and
3. "pattern practice", learning language structure by hearing and replying to brief statements and questions all in the foreign language, thus habituating the properforms.

This enphasis on the spoken language, referred to as the audio-lingual approach is basic to the modern linguistic methods, the rationale for which is in part that it is the first to develop in the life of the child as well as in the history of culture. The consequence of this emphasis in that instruction provide practice in the discrimination and correct production of languages sounds as well as in intonation and rhythm. Failure in these skills results in the familiar foreign accent or brogue. Another basic characteristic of the modern linguistic approach is the attention given to the structure of the language itself, with special emphasis on the structure that differ from those of the native language. As a consequence, the method of instruction is inductive-gradually arriving at rules by a process of generation-instead of deductive, the rules being taught first with the expectation that the student will be able to apply them.

The movement to begin instruction in foreign languages earlier than in the usual high school courses is rapidly gaining headway, and there is already considerable literature on FLES. Because of the nature of young children, the audio-lingual methods tend to be used. Children who come from these classes have difficulty when plunged into high school classes where the old-fashioned, deductive grammatical methods are still in vogue. For this reason, attention is being given to the problem of continuity-opportunity for learners to make continuous progress in the elementary school and high school, and on into college. Such continuity calls for a designation of proficiency in more specific terms than years of instruction. Tests to measure proficiency are being devised, but the task is a difficult one. It involves the measurement of competence in both reception and production of authority and visual symbols. On the reception side it includes sound discrimination, control of grammatical patterns, recognition vocabulary, and reception of context.

More briefly, it requires competence in the ability to read and to understand the spoken language. For production, the competencies are similar-pronunciation. use of grammatical patterns, speaking vocabulary, and conveying of meanings, that is, the ability to speak and write. There is some doubt as to the value of any single proficiency score though a double score for oral and written language might be useful. Any combined score of course, raises problems of weighting of the component items. But any scheme would be better than the present units in terms of duration of instruction.

There are three parts of the complete language laboratory listening station., reproduction area or control room, and monitoring area. The listening stations or positions are small spaces walied up to a height of four feet or so with acoustic materials, and furnished with a chair, table or shelf, earphones, and often a telephone mouthpiece and dialing apparatus for automatic remote control. The student may dial the lesson he is ready for. He listens to the recorded sentences which he "echoes" or answers questions asked, an oral adaptation of the Skinnering teaching machine programme. He may do this through a speaking device so that he hearts himself through his earphones, his voice being amplified so that he hears what he is saying loudly and clearly. His voice may also be recorded and played badk to him for comparison with that of the native speaker. But this proedure, perhaps because of the delay involved, seems as yet to be unnecessarily laborious in view of the results obtained.

The reproduction are is the control room where tapes are stored and played, with the sound funneled to the appropriate booths. The listening stations are situated in the laboratory proper. The monitoring is done either by a teacher moving from booth to booth from a monitoring area or console in the same room, or from a sound-proof room with two-way telephonic transmission. The monitor may be signaled of help, or he can tune in on any lesson to help the student with his difficulties. At the University of Michigan, recordings are being made of the student response that call for monitor interference and also of the assistance provided, in order to study and improve this phase of the instruction.

Hutchinson has summarized the advantages of a good language laboratory. It provides:

1. active simultaneous participation of all students;
2. a variety of native voices, untiring models;
3. for individual differences, lessons adapted to students, which they follow at their own rate;
4. teacher freedom from tedious drilling routines;
5. teacher opportunity to correct students without interupring others;
6. equal hearing conditions for all students;

7. privacy, reduing inhibitions and distractions;
8. facilities for group testing of listening and speaking skills;
9. possibilities for coordinating audio and visual materials; and
10. aid to teachers in improving their audio-lingual proficiency. In addition it provides instruction in languages for which there may be no teacher available, for it is an instructional device, not merely an aid, in that it has direct responsibility for a part in the teaching.

If the audio-lingual method alone is used, those who finish the training have not learned to read and write the foreign language-in this sense they are illiterates. With the traditional course organization, as has best noted, there is no place for them to go, since the usual language classes are made up of students who cannot speak or understand the language and are labouring through the usual rules and paradigms that few native users of the language know. This conditions is being corrected, however, as more and more students have the audio-lingual training. The language laboratory itself is undergoing a transformation in process by becoming a complex teaching machine that will add the reading and writing skills to its repertoire. Already language lessons are being programmed, and it is likely that these skills will be taught much more effectively than they have been in the past.

As is well known, language instruction in America schools has not been given high priority partly because few students had any use for it, and partly because the grammatical methods of instruction, following the Latin model, were unappealing and usually left the student unable either to speak or to read the language. A few were able to translate slowly and laboriously. Even this ability was soon lost through disuse, particularly since only language majors studied any one language more than a year or two, enough to give them the Carnegie units for college entrance-if they went to college.

The emphasis of the linguists and the language laboratories is not on grammar-on declensions, conjugations, and rules. The student does dot learn to *talk about* the language, he learns to use it. Nor is the emphasis on translations. They give primacy to the spoken language on the assumption that people should learn a second or third language in much the same way that they learn their own, first by hearing, followed by speaking, reading, and writing, in that order. The language laboratory at present takes care of the first two stages, although the hearing and saying stages proceed more or less concurrently.

Student behaviour in the language laboratory may be summarized as follows;

Get set: readiness foe the lessons being studied is assured by testing and previous progress, and often aided by preliminary warming up, perhaps including music or pictures from the country that uses the language being studied.

Listen: Language sound, are presented separately, in words, and in sentences.

Discriminate: Differences that make a difference in the new language are emphasized, e.g. Spanish-speaking students learning English may confuse bet and bit; Japanese students lamb and ram, English speaking students the Spanish r, and so on.

Respond: Practice follows in imitating of echoing the foreign sounds, since practically ail of them are different from the English sounds. Verbal instruction can reduce the trial-and-error process here as in other motor skills. Echoing includes practice in intonation, the pitch changes in spoken sentences.

Drill; Responses are repeated over and over in different contexts.

Practice patterns; Lexical meanings are introduced by inserting them in different parts or slots of stock sentences.

Correct through feedback; Throughout, the student compares his pronunciation with that of the recorded voice of the native speaker and, through progressive approximations, relatively quickly acquires the correct pronunciation.

Drill more; The student repeats sounds, words, passages, questions.

Reinforce; Improved and strengthened responses are established as a result of immediate correction, and the attendant satisfaction increases motivation.

Test: *Each response is a test, but cleverly designed paper-and-pencil test reveal the progress each student is actually making.*

Progress; *The student proceeds at his own rate. If he is absent, on his return he begins where he left off.*

Habituate; *Review experiences and continuing effort help the student to make his responses automatic so that he no longer has to think about them but only about what he is saying.*

Naturally these are not to be regards as successive steps but rather as elements of the process that reveals the way in which the language laboratory can follow the learning diagram presented earlier, and systematically build language competence. The meaning of the word course in this connection is understandably vague since the process is continuous, and any break merely signifies that in view of the other things students have to so, progress to some defined point will be expected in a semester or year, though some may reach that point more quickly and others will have to put in extra time, or not cover so much ground. Language learning is basically skill behaviour. A language is a pre-existing structural system to be acquired. There is no occasion for creatively, only for mistakes. The mistakes must be corrected, tight responses taught, habituated, made automatic.

Some say that language skill is not properly viewed as college work, that it is mastered by children in their native country and should be acquired in the elementary and secondary schools, thus leaving instruction in the literature and culture of a country for the colleges to carry on in the language of that country, with minimal attention being given to the language itself. College students who have not attained sufficient competence for such instruction may use the language laboratory until they have, but not for "college credit". Whether or not this goal will be achieved no one can now, It does present a challenge to the schools which now have difficulty in developing competence in their students even in their native language. It is a goal worth striving for and does not preclude the possibility of practice at any level in the expressive use of the language as literature or for acquiring knowledge in any field. But for those purposes, other methods and materials than the present language laboratory will be employed.

Language teachers of the future will need to be better prepared than they are today, but there will be greater satisfaction in leading discussions and reading literature in the foreign language with students who have already mastered the basic auditory and linguistic skills.

Perhaps relatively undue attention has been given to language instruction. But here is where the break-through has occurred. New linguistic procedures and automated techniques make it a special case. It is more than likely that similar advances in other subject will be made. Of course science laboratories, art rooms, shops, and gymnasium have for some time had a place in American schools, but it is doubtful if these facilities have been fully exploited in the interest of effective learning. The mathematics workroom or laboratory is on the way. English, except as it is taught as a foreign language, has yet to profit in any systematic way from the developments in foreign language learning. Social studies as a school subject has had a uncertain career, but the ideals of continuity and proficiency coupled with the potentials of modern technology may produce desirable changes.

Appendix -A

Faced with the choice of craft or profession James D. Finn chose to be a professional. In an age where quality education must be a universal goal; he saw no alternative for the audiovisual educator and educators in general but to move toward becoming professional.

The necessity and vehicle for this move he saw as technology:

1. A technology which is more than invention, more than machines.
2. A technology which is a process and a way of thinking.
3. A technology which increasingly frees man to have greater power to make choices which will control his own destiny.

As a framework for converting a movement into a profession, Finn sets out six characteristics of a profession in 'Professionalizing the Audio Visual field'

1. An intellectual technique.
2. An application of that technique to the practical affairs of man.
3. A period of long training necessary before entering the profession.
4. An association of the members of the profession into a closely knit group with a high quality of communication between members.
5. A series of standards and an enforced statement of ethics.

6. An organized body of intellectual theory constantly expanding by research.

The sixth characteristic he saw as the most fundamental and most important. After examining the status of audiovisual education in terms of each criterion, Finn found it lacking in depth and direction, or 'flying blind." His argument then describes steps which need to be taken before audiovisual education can claim the status of a profession.

The statement, "We need a new audiovisual systems theory; we need it *now*", concludes the articles "AV Development and the Concept of Systems". This predates by about 10 years the surge in the mid-1960s toward the systems approach in education.

Finn briefly describes the "systems concept" and notes its application in industry and the armed forces. He holds that the general theory of educational administration is at least two generations behind the times. This lag has extremely negative effects on the audiovisual field a field which he sees as geared to the technological world of the future with interlocking, complicated systems of men and machines.

Originally made as the president's address to a Department of Audio-Visual Instruction summer meeting in 1960, "Technological Innovation in Education" begins with a reference to King Canute and Ethelred, the Unready. Finn relates these two concepts to DAVI's role in innovation: "We sit on the rising curve of swift technological change in education with some hope of giving it direction."

Finn adds a seventh criterion to the six basic criteria he had earlier discussed for a profession a profession must have the ability to exercise its own leadership. He sees the seventh criterion as based essentially on the sixth, "an organized body of theory constantly expanding by research."

In an examination of the needs and difficulties of innovation and leadership, Finn draws attention to the problem of the "90-day pioneer" who tends after partial success to become orthodox and change resistant.

What does all this mean to the audiovisual profession? As Finn states:

It means, first, that we have to understand and live with accelerating technological change in our own business; it means, second, that we must learn to master these changes and help integrate them into the educational process so that their benefits may be useful and rewarding; it means, third, that we cannot let the practical sociology of the situation deter us or we will lose control of the movement; it means, fourth, that we must lead an intellectually demanding professional life with the forces of technology with which we daily work.

Writing to educators in general through the *NEA journal* in 1960, Finn titled his article "Teaching Machines: Auto Instructional Devices for the Teacher". He stated: "It would help everyone in the teaching profession desiring to assess the teaching machine movement if it were clear exactly what was being talked about, what has been claimed for these devices, what their advantages and limitations are and what they will do and will not do for teachers and students."

The succinct and descriptive article which follows describes teaching machines, theories of programming, types of machines and the state of the art in 1960. The relevance and implications of the technology of individual instruction are outlined in an attempt to help teachers understand and manage instructional technology to further human ends and build teaching into the most human of all professions.

"New Techniques of Teaching for the Sixties" was written principally for those in the field of teacher education. By describing technology as involving systems, control mechanisms, patterns of organization and a way of approaching problems, Finn creates a new perspective for teacher education in the article.

A brief historical overview of developments is provided and the double-pronged growth of "individual instructional technology" and "mass instructional technology" is outlined.

Finn introduces the concept of instructional systems diagrammatically as a combination of individual, mass and conventional instruction.

Four patterns of teacher education in the audiovisual area are identified and discusses. Teachers must consider the implications of technology in education and the need for becoming higher level professionals in order to remain in control of education. "A technology of instruction forces us back to our basic mission-methodology."

"Instructional Technology" was written to support Finn's proposal that DAVI be renamed. The article identifies the high level plateau in the territory the author had spent many professional years mapping and describing so that the profession could reassess, rename and redirect itself toward the future as an integral part of the technological society. "The DAVI that has been my professional life for 25 years must now connect with the future and announce to the world that its members are the technologists of the educational profession."

Seeing the only alternative to looking at the future as looking back at the past, he saw no realistic choice at all. He did not regard the concept of adventurers not the concept of instructional technology as comforting but as essential if we are to keep in touch with the accelerating times and a world of man-machine systems.

"Properly constructed," he wrote, "the concept of instructional or educational technology is totally integrative. it provides a common ground for all professionals, n matter in what aspect of the field they are working, it permits the rational development and integration of new devices, materials, methods as they come along." Finn saw the concept he proposed as a viable alternative to professional splintering and foundering and as a vehicle for professional unity and direction.

In "The Marginal Media Man", Finn seems to be saying that the field is like a supersonic aircraft which has soared up into unexpected air currents and now has spun into control problems for which the crew was not prepared. Lots of potential, lots of success, but lacking direction control was being lost.

"For the plain truth of the matter is that our business, field, profession-whatever you want to call it-is in serious trouble.' Finn re-emphasizes the need to change traditional concepts about the professionalization of the educational media field. 'He saw the media man as always being marginal to many fields.

Finn states the paradox of success and failure, briefly reviews the historical development of DAVI toward professionalism, and examines the current growth and leadership situation. He itemizes publications, convention as, conferences, and councils on the positive side together with the emergence of new technologies, organizations and events such as federal funding. On the negative side of the paradox he makes his case for retrogression of professional development, including the downgrading of the educational media field by the U.S. Office of Education ad the White House Conference on Education that didn't include media.

"A Possible Model for Considering the Use of Media in Higher Education is an edited extract from a memorandum prepared with others for harvard University. The model represents a way of thinking which emerged over a period of time while Finn was working at the national level with professors from several disciplines. He noted how, according to their experience and the structure of their disciplines, the instructors' approach to new instructional processes differed.

Finn summarized that the newer educational media can be applied at several levels-as individual instructional tools, as data storage, for behavior control-type instruction, to build meaning, as research tools, as the core of instructional systems and as a means to increase the distribution efficiency of learning experiences of all kinds.

In "Educational Technology, Innovation, and Title III", Finn records an assessment of Title NDEA funding towards innovation in education. A considerable portion of the original paper, devoted to providing a general context and historical overview is not included because it overlaps other articles in this section. The part used is subtitled "Educational Innovation and Title III" and deals with proposals, confusion of proposal writers, objectives, nature of innovation, hurdles and procedures. Finn states that at federal and state levels there is an attempt through Title III to institutionalize educational innovation through bureaucracies. He notes: "It is still a very moot point whether or not bureaucracy is the exact opposite of innovation."

Other items discussed include scholarly support, dissemination problems and weaknesses or gaps. The article concludes with 11 recommendations.

The closing article in this section is "What is the business of educational technology? Some Immodest Comments on Mr. Muller's Paper". Finn summarizes Muller's argument that educational technology had been oversold at every point along the way; that it had had little effect on the educational enterprise which fundamentally depended upon people, not technology; and that the computer can make contributions to instruction. Agreeing in part regarding the contributions of the computer, Finn then thrusts with the disarming style of an authority at Muller's one sided stance. In refuting Muller's argument, Finn aligns him with the overcautious and pessimistic on the literary side of the Snowian dichotomy.

Citing statistics from data which had been gathered while he was director of the NEA's Technological Development Project, Finn casts doubt on Muller's assertion that technology has had little effect. Emphasizing that the educational system is still highly undeveloped technologically, Finn maintains that we are much further ahead than Muller assumes.

After responding to Muller's categorical statements, Finn goes on to stress the need for instructional technology in today's tri-revolution setting. He raises some questions yet to be resolved regarding the role of the teacher in the classroom, the administrator in the board room and the educator in society. Admitting that educational technology could be used to condition young people to live in a world of standardization, conformity and alienation, Finn stands on the side of mankind ad says we must move towards freedom, creativity and worthwhile sense of self.

Professionalizing the audiovisual field

Specialization of occupation is a growing social factor in modern life. This factor is as applicable to education as to any other field. Once where there only teachers, there are now administrators, psychologists, curriculum consultants, counselors and many other educational specialists. Each of the specialities is developing into a profession with the general profession of education. Educators whose main responsibility lies in the preparation, distribution and use of audiovisual materials represent another group of specialized presonnal newly developed and integrated into the field of education.

In addition to the fact that people working with audiovisual materials are devoting the major share of their time to & specialized phase of education and are developing special interests, techniques, etc., there is also the fact that the audiovisual field itself is somewhat unique in that it embraces all branches of the communication arts and technology and brings new disciplines to bear upon the problems of education. This second fact makes the audiovisual field even more of a specialized educational activity than, say, the teaching of reading.

In recent years audiovisual workers have become sensitive to the professional problems of their specialty. Questions have been raised as to the possible degree of professionalization of the movement; as to what, if any, certification requirement should be set up for audiovisual directors; and as to the long-range professional objectives of associations such as the Department of Audio-Visual instruction of the NEA. DAVI has set up a Committee on Professional Education to study the general problem of professionalization.

It is the purpose of a series of papers, of which this is the first, to present a study of the problem of professionalization to the membership of DAVI from the Committee on Professional Education. These papers will analyze the present status of the field to determine, if possible, the degree of professionalization that has been developed to review the historical development of this status and to suggest some problems that must be met and some possible solutions that might be developed in order to move the field further in the direction of a true profession.

It is hoped that these studies will stimulate the membership of DAVI and other people working in the field to undertake appropriate action. It is very significant to the committee on Professional Education that this series of papers is inaugurated in the first issue of the new professional magazine of the Department of Audio-Visual Instruction.

Tools of a profession

In considering the audiovisual field as a possible area of professionalism, a good place to begin is with the question: What are the characteristics of a profession? A professional has at least these characteristics: (a) an intellectual technique, (b) an application of that technique to the practical affairs of man, (c) a period of long training necessary before entering into the profession, (d) an association of the members of the profession into a closely knit group with a high quality of communication between members, (e) a series of standards and a statement of ethics which is enforced, and (f) and organized body of intellectual theory constantly expanding by research.

The statements identifying these characteristics need little moment. That a profession is primarily intellectual in character can be readily seen by viewing the activities of any profession; a doctor who did not reflectively think before prescribing is inconceivable. That a profession applies its knowledge directly to the benefit of man also obvious.

The long periods of training necessary to develop specialists such as design engineers or oral surgeons are common examples of the third characteristic. Professional associations which began their evolution in the Middle Ages are a part of every civilized society. They identify the members who have successfully passed through the long training stage and in fact, even control to a great degree the nature of that training. communication between members of the profession is carried on by meetings, journals of high quality, consultations, and other means.

Architects, actuaries, engineers all have their codes of conduct or statements of ethics and various forms of standards. Coupled with this ethical formulation is a means of enforcing it in the more highly organized professions. Sometimes this enforcement responsibility rests with the professional association, sometimes with the state as a licensing body and sometimes with both. Although there is much criticism of many professions at this point and some evidence that many codes are window dressing to project the profession from public interference and are not enforced except to the advantage of the profession as against public, the fact remains that the idea of an ethic with power of enforcement places a personal responsibility on each member of a profession not associated with other types of occupations.

Finally, the most fundamental and most important characteristic of a profession is that the skills involved are founded upon a body of intellectual theory and research. Furthermore, this systematic theory is constantly being expanded by research and thinking within the profession. As Whitehead says, the practice of a profession cannot be disjoined from its theoretical understanding, and vice versa. The antithesis to a profession is an avocation based upon customary activities and modified by the trial and error individual practice. Such an avocation is a Craft." The difference between the bricklayer and the architect lies right here.

Professional status of audiovisual education

We can now examine the present status of audiovisual education when measured by these six test of a profession. Are audiovisual personnel, in act, professionals? By audiovisual personnel is mean, for the moment, those individuals who spent 50 percent or more of their time working with audiovisual programs in schools and colleges as directors, supervisors, producers, consultants, etc. or those who engage in in-service and preservice teacher training or research in this area.

An intellectual technique. First, the audiovisual worker does posses an intellectual technique. He has to think reflectively in such varied areas as the critical evaluation of materials, the visualization of abstract concepts, the improvement of instruction and in many aspects of planning and administration. audiovisual personnel as a group, meet this criterion fairly well Practical application of the technique. Second, audiovisual techniques and materials justify their existence only as they become operative in class-room communication. Hence the test of practical application is completely met. Here the personnel of the field is at its best. The practical problems of classroom design, equipment and materials are the meat the drink of most audiovisual people. As will be indicated below, there is, perhaps, even an overemphasis on this point.

Long period of training. The test of a high degree of professionalization of the audiovisual field, however, breaks down completely against the third criterion-a long period of rigorous training for the members of a profession. Most professions not require this long period to training but are also in substantial agreement as to the nature of this training. This results in the professional associations specifying the nature of the training either through state regulation of some sort or through a system of accrediting training institutions.

The teaching profession as a whole does maintain training standards. But specific training for audiovisual directors and other personnel, with few exceptions, is still in the thinking stage. although there have been directors of programs since before World War I, McClusky's bibliography list only 15 articles in the literature which discuss the requirements for audiovisual personnel. An examination of these articles reveals that only four are pertinent. The other are devoted to administrative relationships and duties of principals, building coordinators, students, and miscellaneous problems. There has been practically no thoughtful consideration of this problem by audiovisual people and no attempt to develop standards.

The history of all professions reveals that the lengthy and rigorous training programs came after a long period of evolution. So it is not surprising to find that the audiovisual field has not made an organized effort as yet to develop such a program. The audiovisual field has developed rapidly and has surmounted many professional problems without showing all the required characteristics of a profession. Now, in 1953, the field is really, for the first time, in a position to take good look at the problem of professional training. The State of Indiana has already taken action and proposals have been published in other states as to the training necessary for an audiovisual director and pointing to some form of certification. The Committee on Professional Education of DAVI has this as one of its direct concerns.

The nature and content of professional education for audiovisual directors and other workers present many problems that must be solved before audiovisual education can claim the status of a profession. The system of apprenticeship training that has been in operation is no longer adequate. Trained audiovisual personnel will not stay in their present jobs forever and there is no longer the reservoir of service-experienced people to draw upon. Obviously, a graduate program that can provide the competencies generated by service and industrial experience coupled with a better theoretical background is required immediately. The audiovisual field cannot be upgraded into a profession until this occurs. Other unsolved problems include the nature of certification standards, admissions standards and practices, and placement.

Association and communication between members. The fourth criterion of a profession-a closely knit association with a high quality of communication between members-is another point at which the audiovisual field does not measure up. Considering first professional association, the best that can be said at present is that a professional association is in the process of becoming and will someday emerge.

For many years DAVI was a comparatively weak. organization held together by a small group of stalwarts. DAVI went through several reorganizations and managed to survive a depression and a war, but only in the last two or three years has the organization shown anything like the potential it can develop. The present arrangement which ties in the organization with the NEA through its executive secretary, with working national committees dealing with important problems and with an increasing and interested membership promises much for the future.

The audiovisual field has also suffered from too many organizations. It is a moot question whether the organizations which represent special applications of the field such as The Association for Education by Radio-Television, the Educational Film Library Association, and the Film Council of America should remain outside of the mainstream of the DAVI or become divisions within it in order to develop the best possible organization for the profession. The men and women who founded and carried on these organizations deserve nothing but commendation for their continual struggle and achievements but the field as a profession would probably benefit more by merger than by continued separatism. At least this possibility should be thoroughly explored.

At the state and local levels, the structure of audiovisual organization has not yet even approached the professional. There are some fine state units, to be sure. The Audio-Visual Education

Association of California, one of the oldest and strongest, is a professional organization in every sense of the word. AVID of Indiana has achieved national recognition, and AVDO of Ohio is rapidly growing in strength. And there are others. But much work remains to be done on the state and local levels.

It is at the other half of the concept of association-the idea of a high quality of communication between members-that the audiovisual movement as a whole had failed until the decision was made to publish the journal in which this paper appears. With the exception of Edgar Dale's Newsletter, all of the journals serving the field had difficulty presenting professional content. This was true of Educational Screen, Audio-Visual World, See and Hear, Audio-Visual Guide, Business Screen, The Journal of the AERT, Film News and all the rest. Most of the time these magazines were not able to print through had scholarly papers on the theoretical bases of audiovisual education; research studies for the most part were ignored and left to journals outside the field. When compared to the Psychological Review, The American Journal of Sociology or a hundred other professional periodicals, the audiovisual magazines have simply not measured up professionally. There were good and sufficient reasons for this but the fact remains.

This is not to say that these other audiovisual journals have failed to contribute as the audiovisual field struggled through its infancy. They have done their share in developing the field. In particular, Nelson Greene made a great contribution through the years with the *Educational Screen*. Greene was a scholar and had an intensive interest in professionalizing audiovisual education. Some examples of this interest were the publication of Krows' somewhat dull but important account of the development of the nontheatrical film, carried serially over two years; David Goodman's abortive column on research abstracts, and an attempt to carry a column which critically reviewed the literature of the field.

In general, the journals until now have made a contribution by carrying information on materials and equipment, occasionally publishing an article of professional merit, and everlastingly promoting and crusading for things audiovisual. This is a sign of the childhood and adolescence of the audiovisual movement. Audiovisual education is here to stay. Promotion and professionalization, while both are necessary, are not the same things. The time has come to add the dimension of professional content to the field's journals and it is hoped that the *Audio-Visual Communication Review* will fill the gap.

Professional communication is also carried on in meetings and conference. The same criticisms leveled at the quality of the journals can apply to the quality of most audiovisual meetings. The meeting agenda seem to be of two types. One is a type designed to appeal to the practicing teacher and consists of a rehash of one or more chapters of Dale, Hoban or Kinder carried on for two or three days. To the audiovisual professional, this type of meeting is about as intellectually stimulating as a plateful of unsalted grits would be to Oscar of the Waldorf. The other type appeals to the ever-present gadgeteer in audiovisual circle and, while it may not be concerned any more with the "f-value" of lenses, the topics have merely changed to more efficient booking forms, the JAN projector, or the heat and pressure necessary to laminate a 20 x 24 print.

The writer is not arguing for the elimination of meetings designed primarily for teachers nor for the abolition of the technical problems of the audiovisual field from consideration. Certainly, thousands of teachers need help with the elementary concepts of audiovisual instruction certainly the audiovisual field will always be plagued with technical problems which must be solved. But professional meetings are not professional meetings if they are limited to these two areas. The first can be best dealt with in regular gatherings of teachers rather than at audiovisual meetings and the second area should be reduced to a section or two of professional audiovisual conference to restore perspective.

Again, improvement in recent years has been noted. The agenda for the Boston and St. Louis meetings of DAVI showed many signs of professionalization not present at earlier meetings. Many state meetings have been improving programs. Nevertheless, the improvement of audiovisual conference has a long way to go.

Code of ethics and standards. The fifth measuring point-ethics, standards and their enforcement-is a function of the fourth, a strong association. Statements of ethics and publications. Audiovisual personnel, as members of the teacher profession are subject to the ethics of the profession. As yet, nothing has been done to develop a separate code of ethics for the audiovisual movement.

In the field of standards, there are sings that professionalization is underway. The Committee on Buildings and Equipment of DAVI is studying standards in its field, and has produced and excellent publication.

However, the publication of codes and ethics and manuals of standards in itself guarantees nothing. Professionalization occurs when enforcement is possible and vigorous. Thus, the American Medical Association wages war on quacks and .malpractice; engineers and architects write building standards into the law; and the courts can disbar a lawyer for illegal practice.

Enforcement is closely tied in with admission to the profession by a licensing system, with placement which assures that licensed personnel are hired and most fundamentally, with an obligation on the part of each professional to the ethics and standards of his profession.

In view of the fact that the entire education profession has not met this criterion to the degree that the other professions have, it is questionable whether the audiovisual group will ever completely measure up to this point. And it is even questionable whether such a rigorous arrangement is either necessary or desirable. However, the audiovisual movement will at least have to reach the stage where it has a well-defined code of ethics, a series of standards based upon fundamental research and a form of certification somewhat related to them. At the moment the field is not at this stage and does not meet criterion five.

Intellectual theory and research. As was

indicated in the introductory phase of this paper, the most important characteristic of a profession was the sixth and last-that the technique of a profession is founded upon a body of systematic theory-and research constantly being expanded by research and thinking within the profession. When the audiovisual field is measured against this characteristic, against the conclusion must be reached that professional status has not been attained.

Audiovisual workers have put a premium on "practicality" and have been criticized for this by colleagues within the field of education and by the literati from without. There is some merit to this criticism, For years, even at audiovisual meetings, someone has always taking cracks at the "gadgeteers". As the writer has indicated above, it is his position that the audiovisual field is a result of the fruits of technology applied to the educational process and a certain amount of gadgeteering will always be necessary. Too much, however, reveals a poverty of thought.

The audiovisual field has never been to clear on the point that theory and practice must constantly interact in any intellectual activity of man. In line with some other mistaken educators, many audiovisual people have insisted that they want to be "practical" and not "theoretical", and that "experience" is the thing. This is, in part, an honest reaction against and older viewpoint that placed theory up somewhere near the Milky Way where it has no relation to practice except to cause aesthetic chills to chase up the spine of some professor.

This attitude, however, also represents a complete misunderstanding of the nature of reflective thinking, scientific progress, and the wellsprings of human behaviour. As Dewey has said, "we find that experience when it is experimental does not signify the absence of large and far-reaching ideas and purposes. It is dependent upon them at every point" Without these large and far reaching ideas and field, and this is particularly true of the audiovisual field, can go only so far and then has to stop.

Many of the criticisms listed above are merely symptoms of this greater trouble lack of theoretical direction. Without a theory which produces hypotheses for research, thee can be no expanding of knowledge and technique. And without a constant attempt to assess practice as that the theoretical implications may be teased out, there can be no assurance that we will ever have a theory or that our practice will make sense.

The audiovisual movement is new and growing, but it is in danger of becoming stunted if it is left to its present theoretical formulations. The present theory guiding the movement can be summed up in three references. The basic concept around which all three references. The basic concept arousing which all three have oriented is the notion of the concrete-abstract relationship in learning. This is perhaps most thoroughly explored in Hoban. Dale adds material on retention and forgetting with a brief historical section, and Kinder expands to a very short history of communication and deals slightly with perception and imagery. All also emphasize the gamut of materials approach to learning, the concept of utilization, the experience theory of learning, and the strengths and weaknesses of the various aids.

The remainder of audiovisual theory is scattered throughout the literature. McClusky has related audiovisual techniques to learning theory in a somewhat unique fashion; Brooker began a line of thinking of promise in his discussion of communication which remain to be explored; Exton's contribution of the concept of optimum synthesis" has not received the attention it merits. All of these are but examples of the scattering of notions throughout audiovisual literature which, when brought together, might constitute a beginning of a fruitful theory.

To these examples, of course, much more would have to be added: most of the writings of Hoban, many of Dale's essays in the Newsletter, reports on the proceedings of conferences, generalizations derived from successful practice, generalizations derived from research, etc. The audiovisual field cannot rest its theoretical formulation on the contents of several textbooks designed for teacher training that do not include even all the useful theory to be found in audiovisual literature.

Because of the nature of the audiovisual field, however, useful theory is not confined to its own literature. As most workers realize, there is a literature of the film of photography, of the museum of dramatization, etc.; there is also the literature of educational method and curriculum; there is the literature of educational psychology, of social psychology of social anthropology; there is the literature of art and design; finally and perhaps most important, there is the growing literature of communication. In fact, research and thinking in some parts of the physical sciences the social sciences, and the humanities are each pertinent to the field. We need to understand the filmic expression ideas of Slavko Vorkapich, the visual experiments of Samuel Renshaw and the communication theory of Susanne Langer.

Viewed in this light, most people in the audiovisual field are still guided by a theory which s fragmentary; theory as now guiding the field is not even inclusive of the notions contained in audiovisual literature; it has never worked in most of the pertinent generalizations available from outside these narrow limits.

On the important test of theory the audiovisual field does not meet professional standards. Its workers are craftsmen, not professionals, in the majority of instances because they are operating in Whitehead's words, on "customary activities modified by the trial and error of individual practice." Absolutely fundamental to the development of audiovisual education as a profession in the sense that DAVI is now using the term is the prior development of an all-inclusive body of theory upon which to assess and guide practice and base research. Once this is done many of the other criticisms stated above will no longer be valid because their source will have disappeared.

The status of audiovisual research also reflects on professionalization. Not that research does not exist or that it is not being pursued. A recent bibliography lists 163 titles through 1946, and this is by no means all-inclusive. Because of the journal policy discussed above, research pertinent to audiovisual education is published throughout the literature of the social sciences and reeds a staff of detectives to trace it down. Very little of it has been reported in audiovisual meetings. This means that many audiovisual workers must be "flying blind" a black mark for professionalization.

The post-war years have brought an increase in research activities in audiovisual education and related areas. Much of this research is government sponsored and financed, but it is being published in pamphlet form, is psychological journals, or in other places more or less inaccessible to the practicing worker in the audiovisual field. A true profession, such as medicine, makes this information more easily available to its practitioners. Furthermore, outside of the volume by Hoban and van Ormer, there is not much evidence that research s influencing the formulation of theory. Many of the hypotheses now being tested have been derived from learning theory and the "social perception" theories which have been developed by a number of social psychologists. The audiovisual field is in the peculiar position of having much of its research carried on by workers in other disciplines using hypotheses unknown to many audiovisual workers, and reporting results in journals that audiovisual people do not read and at meetings that audiovisual people do not attend. While the research is expanding the intellectual background of the profession, it seems to be having little effect. A tremendous amount of integration is necessary before this part of the criterion six can be met.

The future of AV Communication

All forms of material progress, including the development of audiovisual techniques and devices for communication, admittedly have brought evil. Material progress and specialization-which is one definition of civilization-have specialization-which is one definition of civilization-have also brought good. A theory of history which can encompass this contradiction in order to help us assess the future, even for the audio-visual field, is all-important. We cannot accept Griswold with his hole in the ground" approach; we cannot accept his ironical suggestion that, in the immediate future, technology will be replaced by mental energy. What then, can we say of our increasingly technical and specialized development in communication that give us guideposts for the future?

Progress, according to this view is not inevitable. As man is increasingly freed by technology and civilization, he achieves a greater power to make a choices which control his own destiny. These choices can be wise or foolish, but it is technology and civilization that give him the opportunity to make them. This view explains why man has, at times in hid development, moved in the wrong direction. Today, we have more choices than ever before; we will probably make more mistakes. But, with Muller, I think that, "Our business as rational beings is not to argue for what is going to be but to strive for what ought to be, in the consciousness that it will never be all we would like it to be "

As whitehead said, "It is the business of the future to be dangerous". Into this uncertainty, into this plural universe where we can make mistakes and intelligent choices, let us project the technological filed of audiovisual communication and apply this theory to three great problems facing our society:

1. The problem of knowledge.
2. The problem of the second industrial revolution.
3. The problem of the public philosophy.

The problem of knowledge

Many dimensions of the problem of knowledge will plague us with communication problems in the future. One of the most difficult aspects of this problem is the fantastic and incredible increase in human knowledge. As the sociologists have told us, we have indeed, invented a method of invention and this method of invention continually spews forth knowledge and information day and night with a double shift working on weekends. For example, the *Quarterly journal of Current Acquisitions* of the Library has received in the fields of science, technology, medicine, and agriculture alone approximately 30,000 journals, including 2,000 new titles; 25,000 research reports; 15,000 books and monographs; 15,000 manuscripts; 10,000 pamphlets, 5,000 prints, blueprints, microfilms, and the like; and 150,000 maps and charts.

The nature of the problem then becomes clear. It would take one person, reading 24 hours a day, approximately 1,00 years to get through the present Yale Library. In the information, at the end of that 1,000 years he would have not made a dent in the then-existing collection. In fact, at the present rate of increases, figuring two hours per book, it would take one person, reading 24 hours a day, approximately two years to read the 15,000 volumes received in the sciences and technology by the Library of Congress during a three-month period. Reading eight hours a day, it would take him approximately six years and that includes Sundays and holidays.

This log jam has to be broken if this knowledge is to be communicated and made useful. It obviously cannot be done by increasing reading speed, desirable as that may be. The world War II Navy slogan for audiovisual materials, "More Learning in Less Time, is one possible approach to this problem. Audiovisual specialists looking toward the future must realize that the next great development of the audiovisual field must be an organized and systematic attack on existing and nascent knowledge so that it may be equipment and personnel that even the dreams of the audiovisual prophets that were so current right after World War II did not anticipate. This is a great social need; our society must meet it beginning now and projecting forever into th future. Money, vision and ingenuity must be continually applied to the communication of knowledge.

The skyrocket growth of the record of knowledge is not, however, confined to books. Each year our films, filmstrips, recordings, charts and kinescopes increases. We are already beginning to meet on a smaller scale the problems faced by book libraries on an extensive scale. The general problem is that when such an extensive record of knowledge exists, how can we locate within this record an item of information we desire? If the existing collection of audiovisual materials is to serve us- if we are to get the right material to the right place at the right time, as so many of us try to do-we must begin not to-do-something about classification, cataloging and location.

The existing film catalogs of libraries; the existing methods used by producers to supply information on new materials; the existing general lists of films, filmstrips and records; the existing methods used by libraries to book and distribute of the 20th century as does the dugout canoe. there are today at least 50 companies that manufacture and instll all sorts of ingenious data-handling equipment used by banks, insurance companies, and scientific institutions. Items can be scanned at the rate of 1,000 a second, digital computers can manipulate records in all sorts of ways. With the exception of a few IBM machines scattered here and there in some of the larger audiovisual departments, nothing has been done in the field of classification, cataloging and location of audiovisual materials that is worthy of this century. We are still publishing catalogs outmoded before they are printed, which grow thicker every year until eventually the post office will have social 10-ton trucks for the delivery of audiovisual catalogs from which will have to order 10 years in advance.

The techniques of the 20th century are now available to help us organize that part of knowledge and information tha exists in the record of audiovisual materials. Where, then are those who are working to code audiovisual materials so that they may be handled under some data processing system? The government-and as Vannevar Bush has pointed out, such general coding is a legitimate task of government-cannot even modernize its postal system where modern data-handling methods could be applied immediately. The comparable to building a house in 1955 out of handhewn logs and tar paper, seems no better able to assist.

And the profession? The profession is always 50 years too late, although a case can be made that the nature of the educational enterprise in this country makes this inevitable. Again, looking to the future , we should set up projects, beginning tomorrow morning, designed to plan, code and introduce modern data-handling procedures into the audiovisual materials system. There is no technical reason, for example , why every teacher in the nation couldn't have almost instantaneous information on any give *scene* in a film, let along the film.

We are also faced with the fact that knowledge, as it becomes more specialized, undergoes continual splintering-a fact which continually worries people concerned with general education. This splintering of knowledge into smaller and smaller compartments has reached the point where information and ideas are no longer being communicated generally among men of learning, not to mention the general public. The ear surgeon cannot speak to the nose surgeon and be understood; the sales tax lawyer can say no more than hello and goodbye to the income tax lawyer; the curriculum director and guidance director cannot even worship Rousseau at the same alter.

This situation, the creation of specialized ignoramuses, so prevalent in America today, is the legitimate concern of President Griswold and many others; for example, his somewhat older compatriot, Robert Maynard Hutchins. Somewhere Mr. Hutchins has said that it would not be necessary to burn the books, only to leave them unread for a couple of generations.

It seems here that the audiovisual field of the future must play a crucial role. We cannot stop specialization for we will stop civilization, whether Mr, Hutchins thinks civilization lies in the great books or not. We must devote much of our future production to the preparation of materials which can generalize knowledge an convey great ideas efficiently and we must devote other production to speeding up and making more efficient communication between groups of specialists. Generalizing ideas, value concepts will not necessarily die if we cannot read all the books. Audio-visual of Bunny Rabbit to such difficult generalizations as, for example, the role of science in society.

Several problems revolving round the concept of the precision of information are also pertinent to our general problem of audiovisual materials and knowledge. Two of these may be described as:

1. Simplification.
2. Information which cannot be coded either into language or pictorial means.

As knowledge increases and becomes more specialized it also becomes more complex. At one time, for example, in the 19th century, Lombrose developed a system of criminology which classified all criminals by facial types and ascribe a biological basis for crime. Today, the cause of crime and the nature of the criminal are known to be extremely complex and possible only of simplification in the tabloid newspapers.

It is in the nature of audiovisual materials to oversimplify many complex ideas an chains of ideas. This is very great danger as knowledge becomes more an more complex. A motion picture is a highly selective device that permits little qualification in its grammar. The users of audio-visual materials in the future will have to handle this difficult problem in the communication situation, or we will indeed, produce a generation with little learning. Producers must face up to the same problem. And the consumer of audio-visual materials must learn to apply the techniques of critical thinking to this type of communication.

You are all familiar with Edgar Dale's "Cone of Experience" or some other concept of the ladder of abstraction of knowledge. All of these ladders put words or language at the top as the most abstract means of communication or formulation of knowledge. We have always assumed, in dealing with audiovisual materials, that, by using these various representations of experience-the film, filmstrip, recording, and the like- that we can help individuals better comprehended what they read by building meaning into abstractions.

This idea that words are the most abstract containers of knowledge is now a more or less false idea. Above words, exist as a higher order of abstraction that comes more and more into use as this century progresses. I refer to mathematics. There are now many concepts impossible to describe except mathematically. Language will not do.

Precisely what this development means, I am not at this time prepared to say. Certainly, it should make us more humble toward the possibility of communicating all pf knowledge by audiovisual means in the future. While, for example, the concepts of entropy may be visualized, they may not be visualized in the mathematical sense and they cannot be stated in language, and here I am certain that even Dr. Griswold's ESP will not help us much. The problem of the formulation and communication of knowledge is vast; we must be prepared, in the future, to question a number of assumptions regarding audiovisual materials that are accepted without question today; basic here is the concrete-abstract relationship.

There is also a possibility inherent in the great ability of audiovisual materials to simplify and to communicate efficiently that can make the future of knowledge dark instead of bright, terrifying instead of hopeful. I refer here to the fact that audiovisual communication techniques can be used in the future to prevent knowledge and information to immoral ends, This is the last dimension of the problem of knowledge that I wish to consider.

In science fiction as has been demonstrated over its long history, we can find great artistic instights into the possibilities of the future. Throughout modern Utopian science fiction, as handled by the greatest writers, runs a common, horrifying thread. This thread can be found in Huxley's *Brave New World*, in Orwell's 1984, in Ray Brandbury's

Fahrenheit 451, and even in such a short a short story as Henry Kuttener's incredible. "Year Day." This threat is also present in the writings of philosophers. Bertraned Russell considers the possibilities of the scientific totalitarianism of the future which may come into existence if we make the wrong choices.

The common thread of horror as seen by these insightful artists is that the mass communication media-audiovisual media for the most part-may in the future be the means by which society is conditioned both in school and out for life in a totalitarian regime. Audiovisual materials are the ideal means for this. With them, we can truly convince that black is white, that Big Brother is all good, that humanity is worthless. With these materials, we can make all good, that humanity is worthless. With these materials, we can make all of society into in vast Pavlov's dog, conditioned to accept whatever it sees and hears as true knowledge and to salivate at the will of its director. It is entirely possible with the right controls to pervert knowledge and control information with audiovisual materials.

This, you may say, is not the concern of audiovisual people. You may say that out job is to take the materials as developed and see that they are usod. This point of view I would call the transmission-belt concept of the audiovisual mission and I will not accept it. If the job of audiovisual people is merely to transmit materials, if we turn our minds and energies to it, we can all be replace by electronic computers in 10 years-computers that can do out jobs much more efficiently.

I submit that it is our job to be concerned about the content and philosophy of the materials we use in the future. I agree with the anthropologist, Redfield, who, in recently

discussing the scientific method with hi colleagues, said, "Just who are you neutral for?" And he answered this question,..." I have placed myself squarely on the side of mankind and have not shamed to wish mankind well".

Already there are signs that pressure groups, government officials at various levels and various people with axes to grind, desire to step in and control the audiovisual materials we use in the schools. The films of my good friend, Lester Beck ,cannot be used in a school system not far form here, due to the efforts of an interesting combination of pressure groups. In the same system, great pressure is put on th audiovisual department to list the programs of a reactionary radio commentator in a radio-listing bulletin for schools and to eliminate naming any liberal commentators whatsoever. This is the beginning of 1984 in 1955. in the public arena, we have in existence phony television forum programs and allegedly impartial magazines which are elevating the perversion of information into a fine art.

If we are on the side of mankind ; if we believe that the future must contain choices, we must, in the future, defend the freedom of audiovisual communication and see that the materials contain, insofar as it is possible, all knowledge, not a perversion of it.

As I have tried to show, then the problem of

knowledge, it terms of its scope, in terms of its organization, location and distribution, in terms of its increasing specialization, in terms of conveying it precisely, and in terms of its possible audiovisual are all intimately connected with the future of audiovisual communication. The problem of knowledge is one of the greatest out society must carry into the future; it is an absolute social necessity that we begin now to apply audiovisual techniques to aid in its solution, and to protect its integrity.

The problem of the second industrial revolution

Knowledge and technological civilization are tow sides of the same coin. Technological civilization has been the product of the Industrial Revolution. Today we are told that we are in the beginning stages of the Second industrial Revolution. Two factors are making this possible-atomic energy and automation.

Atomic energy, in its peacetime aspects, will helps us do better the world's work. Automation, while ostensibly also helping us with the world's work, will apparently redesign the world in which we live. Automation is simply defined as the use of machines to run machines. Electronic computers and other forms of control mechanisms now make it possible to move materials to a machine, control the machine, and keep track of its production. Feedback of information at all points keeps the system running.

A complete automobile engine can not be made, it is said, untouched by human hands in a sort of push-button factory controlled by electronic brains. Application of the process is seen in oil refineries; pipelines, and even in forestry.

However, as Peter Drucker has recently pointed out, automation is not a menials, machine-operated production. Its primary characteristic is a process- a way of thinking involving patterns and self-regulation. It is here that the educational implications are tremendous. Automation is not simply a problem of technological unemployment or employment. To quote Drucker Automation's most important impact will not be on employment but on the qualifications and functions of employees"

This means that very large numbers of workers of high technical skill will be needed to create maintain and control the machines. More important, large numbers of managers will be required to operate the process-to think to analyze to decide. Some economists feel that another complete upgrading of all workers is absolutely necessary to run and automatized world. The peasant, with his wooden hoe, was once upgraded into a semi-skilled factory worker over along-long period of time. The factories and offices of tomorrow will need higher-grade employees to be created immediately-employees working under a system which makes possible the human use of humans beings.

In order to avoid technological unemployment, it is the best estimate of many familiar with the situation that much of our labor force will have to be retrained quickly for new jobs; that much of the future labor force will have to be provided with the kind of generalized education required to produce men capable of high-level analysis and synthesis; that th increased use of leisure time- the 30-hour week is not far off- will demand a change in all Edcuation.

Audiovisual materials may be the only answer to the retraining problem-audiovisual materials created and used jointly by the schools, industry and labor unions. The estimates of the number needing such training run into the millions. The speed needed approaches that of World War II. If this hypothesis is true, the future demands on the audiovisual field will be fantastic.

The type and use of audiovisual materials in the schools of the future to educate young people to live and participate productively in the society created by the Second Industrial Revolution will have to be much different. The curricular implications are clear. Life Adjustment a curriculum movement which is already being questioned in some quarters, in my opinion will be dead as the dinosaur.

The creeping control of the emotional "Rousseauians" over all levels of education will be halted and restored to its proper perspective. We are on the edge of an era requiring an iron content in cur education-whether the curriculum supervisors and some of their audiovisual worshippers are ready for it or not. This content will by no means be the same as the much maligned subject matter of yesteryear and so will give scant comfort to Professor Bestor and other critics but it is also certain that it will not consist of courses in how to paint your house. New audiovisual materials must be created and used to carry this content. It was not easy to move the peasant with his hoe to the level of a machine tender, it will be more difficult to make the next move, upgrading the entire intelligence and achievement of the American people. We will have to do it, and audio-visual materials are our best bet to help us.

The problem of public philosophy

In *The Public Philosophy*, Lippmann traces the causes of the decline of the Western democracies to the disintegration of the public philosophy-our general traditions of government and civility. One reason for this decline, he suggests, is due to the fact that we have not remade this public philosophy-the glue that holds us all together-to fit the times; another reason is that, through a mistaken theory of education and a general surrender of the communication media to trivia, we have not communicated the public philosophy. His remedies lie in the reverse of this process-the remaking of our traditions of civility to fit the times and the rebuilding of an educational and communication system that will communicate them.

Mr. Lippmann's position in *The Public Philosophy* has been soundly criticized. I am inclined to agree with some of these criticisms, particularly those that point out that his analysis is principally based on European experience. At times, one wonders whether or not Mr. Lippmann really knows the United States at all. However, his thesis that a public philosophy adequate for the times needs to be communicated throughout our society is very sound.

This, it seems to me, is the final and great challenge for the audiovisual movement in the future. We can well disintegrate without blowing ourselves up in an atomic flash. We can become so immersed in trivia that a scientific dictatorship is inevitable. With an adequate and adequately communicated public philosophy made possible, in part, by the intelligent use of the audiovisual media of communication, we can survive to look forward problems grew, there evolved throughout the organization the concept of a system. By this he meant that the drone radioplane could not be considered separately. Everything associated with it had to be developed, studied or taken into account. This meant that the company designed launching platforms for special uses on land and sea; it manufactured recovery vehicles; it developed a system of repair and maintenance and spare parts service; it developed a training program and trained Armed Forces personnel; it gathered a staff of field men; it geared its research and development program to that of the Armed Forces.

Now, what the Army or Air Force was buying from this manufacture was not a radio target plane. The Army cr Air Force obtained, with the contract, a system of radioplane use from the means for getting the plane in the air to the means for recovering and repairing it. This *system* of radio target plane use was integrated, in each of the Armed Forces, into other systems to create a working efficient organization.

Here is the lesson that school administrators and audiovisual directors must learn-the lesson of the modern concept of systems. A little inquiry will reveal that the systems concept is one of the hottest ideas now occupying the attention of top industrial management, industrial psychologists, the Armed Forces and many others. The systems concept, while certainly now new, has evolved into a major corollary of the premises of automation. It is related to "operation analysis" or "operations research", as these terms are used to refer to management techniques now being studied and applied in the Armed Forces and in certain advanced segments of industry.

Essentially, the systems concept is an idea of organization. It is an idea of organization that includes what might be called the gestalt or whole function of a unit or organization. Thus, in advanced management research circles today, "men-machine systems" and "machine systems" are carefully set up and studied, When an aircraft-bomber or commercial-is in the air, it consists of an intricate system of men and machines made up of smaller unit systems of men and machines. To make that aircraft accomplish its objective-whether to deliver a bomb or a sack of mail-it is necessary that the system as a whole be managed. What is important is not the physical and psychological condition of the pilots, the electronic devices, the code used with the tower, *each taken separately but the gestalt or field* of all these items and many more, *considered as they interact with each other in a system.*

We hold that the general theory of educational administration is years behind that of modern management. How many years, it is difficult to say. About two generations would probably be a good guess. The theory of educational administration is still occupied with bits-with atoms and pieces. The present theory of educational administration confines itself to such things as the problems of line and staff organization. For example, we know of a new junior college in the process of organization.

The director of instruction set up a job on the chart for a audiovisual director-a professional persons. But the college had a consultant-a well-known theorist in educational administration. When the consultant got through with the organization chart, the audiovisual director was gone and in his place, a great concession was made with the substitution of an audiovisual technician-a projector repairman, if you will. It can easily be shown that with that one move, the audiovisual potential of the instructional program was reduced 100 percent. Classroom efficiency went out the window in return for what appeared to be an "efficient" organization chart. The audiovisual program of the college was simply not considered as the system it is.

We do not imply here that this is an isolated case or that the administration theorist was acting either maliciously or with caprice. He was, as a matter of fact, acting consistently within the best form of thinking abroad in educational administrative circles today. The point is that this thinking is at least two generations behind the times and it is for this reason, among others, that the audiovisual movement never gets off the ground.

For an audiovisual program-and this is the heart of our argument-is a clear-cur system. The system begins with the production of materials-films, per-recorded tapes, or even a classroom bulletin board-and ends with the recovery or replacement of the materials. It is a man-machine system. Involved, within the school situation, are people-teachers, administrators, students, clerical, and technical help; materials, machines, other systems, and outside institutions-dealers, producers,

What is the value of this concept of audiovisual administration as a system,? It should, for example, stop immediately the wasteful practice engaged in by some schools of putting the materials in one location under the supervision of a "materials" person and the equipment under the supervision of another leaving the teacher to do the coordinating. This is no system; this can be chaos, although it looks "efficient" on an organization chart-not so many "unproductive" personnel.

The concept of an audiovisual system would also reduce the ridiculous lack of coordination which results in building classrooms with no light control on the one hand and investing in projectors and materials on the other. If there were no other fact in existence to establish that present-day administrative theory and practice is an automistic, old-fashioned,outmoded business, this fact would do it. If, instead of considering buildings in the category of "buildings" and audiovisual materials and devices in the category of "curriculum materials," administrators were, for five minutes, to consider the audiovisual program as a system, obviously lighting, ventilation and even proper bulletin board and chalkboard space would be related to the problems of teacher use of these materials. Buildings would be built with the system in mind.

Equipment is another example. According to recently released National Audio-Visual Association figures, the number of 16mm motion picture projectors produced in the U.S. in 1954 was 10,000 less than the number produced in 1947. Granted that in the early post-war years it was necessary continuing production since that time has put a lot of projectors in the field, the fact remains that this is a bad sign for development of the audiovisual movement to a freer and happier life.

This has been my theory of history as it frames the future of audiovisual communication. The future presents us with the picture of an incredible load of knowledge, a radically new social organization, and a necessity to communicate the public philosophy. ESP will not handle these problems at all; Dr. Griswold's books can make some contribution; audio-visual communication, I am convinced, must carry the major share of the load into the future-the future which will always contain the contradictory elements of good and evil-between which we must always make difficult and constantly more intelligent choices.

14 Technological Innovation in Education

There were, in Holinsheds time, at least two different versions of the story of Canute and the sea. The heritage that has come down to us, however, is contained in the bare bones of the story-the futility of man commanding the sea to stand still. One does not have to be an historical determinist to accept the point. If old Canute had wanted to do something about the tide, he could at least have built a sea wall.

Canute wrested control of Britain from Ethelred, the King of Wessex. Some authorities called him Ethelred, the Unready; others, Ethelred, the Redeless- meaning a man who lacks counsel. Again, however, using Marshall McLuhan's concept of the bare bones of a code surviving subsequent changes in culture, the stark idea of ordering the sea to turn back and the equals stark idea of defeat because the leadership was unready appeal to me as a way to start thinking about the problem of technological innovation in education.

Actually, I am indebted to Francis Noel for the suggestion that this subject be examined in some detail. Last winter, at the state meeting of the Audio-Visual Education Association of California.

Francis, in a brief speech, uttered a warning to the membership that they were running the risk of becoming fact and lazy on the job right in the middle of the greatest tide of technological change ever to hit the audio-visual movement-right at the time when they should be lean, hard and hungry. In such a context I would like to discuss DAVI, our own national organization. We must, I think, raise the question as to what is the role of such an organization in this era of swift change in our own business.

DAVI is now very important. As a group of people working with modern communication devices in education, we find suddenly that there is great national and international interest in what we do and say. We find many other groups either asking us for help or counsel, or invading our territory. The professional educator, the school board member, the PTA, the news media, politician and taxpayer groups, and even the critics of education have all suddenly discovered instructional technology and, consequently, DAVI. Incidentally, this sudden importance poses many internal problems which it is going to take us several years to solve. Our immediate problem, however, is to assess this importance-which of course, we always felt we had-in more general terms.

The basic reasons for this interest are known to all of you. They are rooted in the twin explosions of population and knowledge, in international tension, in the teacher shortage, in the lack of facilities and so on. Fundamental to all of these, however, is the fact that technological change-partly as an effort to solve some of these problems and partly by its very nature of constant expansion-has invaded all of education to the point where it is inescapable.

There is no doubt in my mind that we have broken through the "oat barrier" in education. This means that each successive development will take effect in a shorter time than the last one. Compare, for example, the rate of acceptance of the sound film sixth television. Ten years after the introduction of sound motion pictures into education there were film libraries that were not buying a single print of a sound motion picture, so convinced were they that silent film was as far as education ought to go.

Television has caught on much more quickly and with wider effect. I would predict that, other things being equal, teaching machines will outstrip television as to rate of integration into the educational system. The problem of programming, seem as a great deterrent just a few months ago, seems much closer to solution. One large educational film producer, for example, has five teams of programmers in the field turning out material with great rapidity. A school in new York that has experimented a great deal in this field is setting up a general programming service. our curve is going up right beside the transportation curve. I hate to speculate on what might be possible with 8mm sound film at this point in time.

The second element of importance in technological change is that it is cumulative. Consider the automobile. C.L. McCuen of the General Motors Research Laboratories noted a few years ago that:

The automobile is the modern version of a road

vehicle first built by the French engineer Cugnot in 1969. It is Otto's contribution of the four-cycle engine. It is the basic electrical discoveries of Henry, Faraday, Ampere, Volta and Benjamin Franklin. It is Kettering's self-starter and Thomas Midgley's tetraethyl lead.

In this second element we find the explanation for the first-the speed of change. Cumulation has affected the audio-visual technological complex to such an extent that, today, we are, willy-nilly, in a new phase-as when water suddenly turns to steam, to borrow from Willard Gibbs by way of Henry Adams.

The nature of this change, then, presents the basis problems of people who are organized together to promote the technology of instruction. And I must insist that going back to the Keystone slide sets and streographs at the turn of the century, this is what the audio-visual field has always been about. We have been attempting to introduce and to manage instructional technology; this term of course, must be broadly defined; it includes the systems involved, the methods of use, the learning research which supports it, the measured reactions of social groups to media and many other elements.

This wave of technological change, like the waves of Canute, will not go away. One of the problems I have faced as president of DAVI is that, by the mere process of calling attention to these overwhelming facts, I have been shot at, verbally, even by some of our own members. It have been suggested, for example, that we should forget about teaching machines on the grounds that they are primarily verbal devices-in the face of evidence that some of the better machines use audio-visual methods of presentation and of the more fundamental fact that these technological devices will obviously be treated within the school and college situation as are the other "teaching machines" such as the motion picture projector, the television receiver and the tape recorder.

With the more general audiences of teachers and administrators, the unrest is even greater. I have been accused of inventing the vacuum tube and the transistor in order to replace teachers. I wish, I had invented these devices; having missed that opportunity, I can only assure the threatened educators that they will not go away. Our problem remains as I have stated it before: "...not so much of how to live with on some kind of feather-bedding basis, but how to control it so that the proper objectives of education may be served and the human being remain central in the process"

A profession of innovators

Within this pattern of unrest and change and desire of some people to order the waves to stand black, what is the role of DAVI? More generally, what is the role of an organization of educational innovators?

I think we have, to begin with a realistic assessment of the nature of our membership and of our organization. Any organization such as ours is a conglomerate sum of a professional association, a learned society, a trade union, a trade association and some kind of a social group within which we can carry on shop talk. Our members include full-time teachers who are personally interested in the use of audio-visual materials or who are in charge of a program for their department or building, college professors who do research in this field, administrators of audio-visual service programs large or small, producers of materials from graphic to television programs, psychologists, curriculum specialists, librarians government information specialists, broadcasters, military and religious audio-visual people-and many others. We are conglomerate in both purpose and membership and yet, as a whole, with this mutual interest in a field almost impossible to define, we sit on the rising curve of swift technological change in education with some hope of giving it direction.

If I were to sum up the meaning of this description of the membership of DAVI and its organization, I would have to say that we are moving in the direction of becoming a true professional organization of extreme importance to education and to America. We have a long way to go , but not as far as we did in 1952 when, as some of you know, I attempted to make as assessment of our status as a profession.

At that time, I examined the Davi Situation using six criteria usually accepted as measuring the degree of professionalization of a group of workers. I am interested here only in exploring further the sixth criterion which stated that a profession had "an organized body of intellectual theory constantly expanding by research" . To this, I would like to add a seventh, namely, that a profession must have the ability to exercise its own leadership.

To some, the idea that a profession must exercises its own leadership may sound like a contradiction in terms. A little thought, however, will reveal that all professions, one way or another, tend to turn into priesthoods. And, long ago, William James said that a priesthood never initiates its own reforms. To some degree, this has happened with the audio-visual field. We must face the brute fact that many of the recent innovations giving us headaches today have been forced upon us from the outside. I would be the first to say that this has, by no means, been entirely the fault of the audiovisul profession. Some of this short circuiting has been deliberate on the part of outside agencies for other purposes; some has been the result of technological accident-an invention or process just turns up and people outside of our group begin to work with it.

Other audiovisual innovations taken over by, offered to or otherwise passed on to groups outside the mainstream of the audiovisual movement have ended up where they have because individual members of our profession have refused to see the relevance of these innovations in the pattern of instructional technology. A recent historic example-recent enough to have occurred within the last 20 years and yet illustrative Exactly 20 years ago at a DAVI meeting in connection with the NEA summer convention, a discussion was held as to whether or not we should change the name from the Department of Visual Instruction to the Department of Audio Visual Instruction. It was suggested that the time was ripe as the people interested in educational radio and recording were then meeting to discuss the formation of what was later called the Association for Education by Radio.

I'll never forget the remark of an audiovisual

director who said, "What are we talking about radio and recordings for? I have enough to do just keeping up with films put out by Encyclopaedia Britannica and Coronet". There was other opposition, too and we remained DVI for some years after that. The members of the organization refused to take the responsibility for their own leadership. True, we were small, weak and scattered. But perhaps that's why we remained so for much longer than necessary.

I should to emphasize that this business of exerting leadership depends primarily upon the sixth criterion-an organized body of theory constantly expanding by research. no one, no profession, no organization can seize the present and bend the future to proper ends without it. We must know our own posture; we must know where we want to go and why. In an intellectual field, this becomes a demanding intellectual problem placing constantly higher requirements upon our members. The way of the innovator is hard.

The practical sociology of innovation

If intellectual demands make the life of the innovator difficult, what I call the "practical sociology of innovation" makes it even more so. Actually, in the audiovisual movement we face two problems of innovation simultaneously. The first-and this is more of a problem than even before-is resistance to innovation by our own members. Some of them are playing Canute and Ethelred, the Unready, at the same time; they wan the waves to stand still and they're not ready to deal with the when it keeps rolling in.

Second, we always have been to some degree, the innovators of the educational profession. This is because we have always been the technologists of learning and in our society, the technologist is the innovator. Some of our members remember the time when they has to go out and sell the idea of using a motion picture in the classroom' and in many places it was about as easy as selling MR. Khrushchev on subscribing to a U-2 photographic service. As a matter of fact, this idea of using films extensively in teaching is by no means completely sold to the whole of American education to this day.

It should be obvious that we cannot develop new ideas and processes within all of American education until we first learn to live with change and innovation within our own professional segment. We are in danger I think, of developing an audiovisual orthodoxy-which was, what Francis Noel was worried about in Sacramento last winter. We have too many people who are what might be called 90-day audiovisual pioneers. That is, for a time they were out in front of education waving the banners for a film libraries, tape recorders, central sound systems, or the concept that the concrete is better than the abstract. But pioneering is hard work and many people don't care to stay with it for much longer than the proverbial 90 days. And so, some of four friends stopped pioneering as soon as they acquired a little living space, status or an Instructional materials center. And they became orthodox and fat, and change-resistors. Worse, some of the stopped thinking, worrying and wrestling with the problems of the swiftly developing instructional technology. This is part of the practical sociology of innovation. It hurts more right now because we happen to have hit one of those swift-rising audiovisual cycles.

Another aspect of the sociology of innovation is at the opposite pole. we can have too much novelty, too much change which is neither useful nor ornamental. Hardy-Cross, the famous engineering professor at Yale, once gave the engineers some advice that applies as well to us. He said:

The problems of today are in many respects the problems of hundreds of years ago, but these problems deal sometimes with new materials and always with different conditions. When a problem is all solved and the answer is very definitely known in the field of engineering, it is about time to investigate that problem again, because what is known is probably known for certain limited materials. But novelty should not be pursued for itself alone. The novelty often consists in merely doing another thing in about the same way that other things have been done before.

We don't need orthodoxy, but we do need the law of conservation of audiovisual energy. We need hard thinking, based upon our general intellectual posture, as to which is baby and which is bath. We also do not need any additional self-anointed experts springing from nowhere to lead to charge for a fad which, for a few short months or a year or two, makes them into some kind of local savants. This matter of conservation, distinguishing dross from gold, is also part of the practical sociology of innovation.

Innovation of certain kinds is highly rewarded. Not so with educational innovation; in many cases the educational innovator is punished. I know personally, for example, of a friend with a reputation as an educational innovator who was blocked from a large an important job merely because he had carried out his ideas. Other friends have been castigated by their colleagues and have been denounced in professional circles for the same reason. Until such time as educational innovation is justly rewarded, the practical sociology works against us. The network of groups back of the educational innovator is not necessarily one to which he can turn for approval. This is a great deterrent to us in our business of educational innovation.

Innovation and cultural change

Instructional technology, which has become the major basis for educational change now and in the foreseeable future, also presents us with professional problems at a level, somewhat higher than that of practical sociology. I refer to the fact that the kind of innovation we are facing in the American culture as a whole and in our specific educational culture is of such a nature that it can change these cultures overnight.

When we consider the audiovisual segment of education and the new media with which we deal, the words of Marshall McLuchan are as plain:

The children of technological man respond with untaught delight to the poetry of trains, ships, planes and to th beauty of machine products. In the schoolroom, officialdom suppresses all their natural experience; children are divorced from their culture. They are not permitted to approach the traditional heritage of mankind through the door of technological awareness; this only possible door for them is slammed in their faces...

Photography and cinema have abolished realism as too easy; they substitute themselves for realism.

All the new media, including the press, are art forms that have the power of imposing, like poetry, their own assumptions. The new media are not ways of relating us to the old "real" world; they are the real world, and they reshape what remains of the old world at will.

Official culture still strives to force the new media to do the work of th old media. But the horeseless carriage did not do the work of the horse; it abolished the norse and did what the horse couls never do. Horses are fine. So are books.

Technological art takes the whole earth and its population as its material not at its form.

It is too late to the frightened or disgusted, to greet the unseen with a sneer. Ordinary life-work demands that we harness and subordinate the media to human ends.

If, as a profession with education, we are to control the new instructional technology, we must realize and live with this fundamental fact of cultural change. It should be neither a surprise nor the crack of doom to us that the role of teacher will probably change drastically in the future; it should be a challenge to solve the problem so that the nation, the students and the profession will all benefit.

To use another example, there is no question in my mind that we cannot afford to retain an orthodox position on reading instruction. The culture has changed. Children are beginning school after six years of adult education presented then by television, motion pictures, radio, advertising and a host of other media. Their vocabularies are simply not those discovered by Throndike and others years ago. Their stock of meanings has changed. This probably implies a new system of reading instruction involving audiovisual approaches, phonetic analysis and yet-undiscovered methods; it certainly does not mean the slow addition of 150-200 words a year.

What, then, does all of this mean to the audiovisual profession? It means, first, that we have to understand and live with accelerating technological change in our own business; it means, second, that we must learn to master these changes and help integrate them into the educational process so that their benefits may be useful and rewarding, it means, third,that we cannot let the practical sociology of the situation deter us or we will lose control of the movement; it means, fourth, that we must lead an intellectually demanding professional life in order to deal with the forces of technology with which we daily work.

Finally, it means that we should remember the words of Edgar Dale from a recent article in which he said:

The disease in all professions is stagnation, a failure to grow in professional wisdom and competence. The curve of growth is not typically a constantly rising line, but one in which plateaus are soon reached. We wonder why children don't want to learn, yet their teachers may exemplify persons who have stopped learning, who have little feeling of the need for disciplining themselves to high standards or professional excellence.

DAVI, it is turns out to the nothing else, must be an organization of innovators. In it we need no Canutes; more important, we can have no Ethelreds who are unready. The way of the innovator can be exciting, if hard.

Teaching machines

The american teacher may soon need a new professional dictionary. These days an auto-instructional device is not an Aetna Driver Trainer. A motion picture projector, contrary to what may be thought, is not a teaching machine. reinforcement is not something you put in concrete or bring up to save the Lost Battalion and programming does not refer to they way a conductor sets up a concert or an adviser a series of courses for a student.

These terms and some others like them-"repertoire", for example-have been invented or adapted to be used in the new field of teaching machines, self-instructional devices, or auto-instruction.

Because of the national publicity some of the experiments with automated instruction have achieved, teachers are naturally concerned with these developments and are raising many questions. It would help everyone in the teaching profession desiring to assess the teaching machine movement if it were clear exactly what was being talked about; what has been claimed for these devices, what their advantages and limitations are and what they will do and will not do for teachers and students.

What is teaching machine?

A teaching machine or auto-instructional device is a piece of apparatus designed to be operated by an individual student. There are many types and varieties of teaching machines, but all of them have the following characteristics in common;

1. The student is presented with a question or problem by some form of display on the machine.
2. The student is required to respond *overly*- that is, be must do something about the problem such as writing an answer or pushing a button to indicate an answer.
3. The student is informed, one way or another, as to whether his answer is right or wrong and in some cases, why he is right or wrong.
4. Often an account is kept of the response to each item-not for testing purposes, but for teaching purposes ass for example, when the machine has a provision to repeat items that have been previously missed.

The device per se is not important except as a vehicle for the program, which is the heart of the auto-instructural concept.

The content to be taught is analyzed and developed into a program. The program is the series of items which is presented to the student in the form of questions, problems, blanks to be filled in pictures and diagrams to respond to and so forth.

Programs are designed, taking into account a theory of learning, the nature of the student for which the program is being designed, the subject matter to be worked on, whether or not a teaching machine will be used to present the program, and the capabilities of the particular machine, if open is to be used.

Theories of programing

Perhaps the foremost theory of programing in vogue among research workers today is one which requires that the student construct his own response.

This is usually done to exposing to the student a question or problem which contains a blank covering one or more words.

The student is required to write these words, not in the blank itself, but on a piece of paper in another part of the machine. One he has committed himself, he operates a lever or button which exposes the correct answer and at the same time, moves his answer under a piece of glass or plastic so that he can compare but not change.

Teachers must remember that we are dealing here with hundreds or even thousands of discrete, interlocking stops to be worked on by the student over a period of time so that he may learn-in the case of constructed response programs-certain kinds of verbal behavior.

Items repeat, come at the student form different directions and constantly add to his store of information and vocabulary. The programs, if its is a good one, starts where the student is and gradually leads him into unknown territory by short enough jumps so that, theoretically, he never makes a mistake..

At this point in the constructed response program, several things can happen, depending upon the kind of machine used. Uncertain devices, the items the student answers correctly are dropped any only those he missed reappear. In others, there are self-scoring provisions where he can punch a paper tape on which he has written his answers so that his errors are recorded. In still others, an intermediate stage is exposed, giving the student additional prompts before revealing the whole answer.

Another from of machine uses a multiple-choice approach to programing. Here the student is presented with a classical multi-choice question which contains some prompting information as well. He responds by pushing a button beside the proper number, pushing a pencil through a special hole etc.

The primary difference is that this program require a different type of responses from the student- a reaction to alternatives rather than the construction of an answer. While the difference between these two types of programming may seem superfical, a certain amount of controversy exists in psychological circles over the relative merits of each.

A third form of programming involves what is called "branching". In devices incorporating branching techniques, if the student makes a mistake, the machine may take him off the main track of the program onto a "branch ' in order to build up information or background before he returns to the main program.

In a sophisticated machine, branching also permits a bright student to move ahead rapidly after he has demonstrated competence by answering a certain number of questions correctly. Again, because of field is so new, there are proponents and opponents of the branching-type program.

So far, all the programs mentioned have been concerned will verbal behavior-the use of words and abstract concepts. However, there is nothing intrinsic in any of the three types of programming described which confines them to verbal patterns alone.

Construction problems can be based on pictures, maps, charts and diagrams. The same thing is true of multiple-choice programing. Intrinsic or branching programing in one current machine makes us of short motion picture sequence.

Recent developments in the field indicate that audiovisual approaches will enter more and more into the teaching machine and hence, the programming picture. Experiments have been made , for example, with motor-skill teaching. Machines now exist using slides and tapes and motion pictures.

While the basic programing techniques used with these audiovisual stimulus materials may be one or combinations of the three programing theories just described, the introduction of these nonverbal materials will probably led to still other forms of programming.

Types of machines

In order to reach the student with the program, various kinds of technological arrangements are being experimented with. These are the teaching machines referred to in the first section and the programmed textual material which will be discussed later.

Auto-instructional devices exist in a wide range of technological sophistication. This range includes no machine at all- for example, merely a set of cards in a cardboard or plastic case, or a mimeographed sheet; a write-in machine: a machine using slides and tape; a multiple-choice machine: a film machine; a machine using a combination of microfilm and motion pictures; and a set of machines electronically tied in with a television broadcast.

In addition to the machines, two kinds of textual material are now available that make use of programing concepts. One is the programed textbook, in which the items are presented much as in a construction machine with the answer usually on the page following the item.

The other is called a scrambled textbook. Here the next makes use of the branching technique. The student begins and after some instruction, works a problem with a multiple choice answer.

Each of the choice directs him to a different page in the book. If he is correct, on a page he turns to he finds more instruction and another problem. If he is incorrect, he is directed to a different series of pages depending upon the nature of his error. Both of these textbooks are different from traditional workbooks and should not be confused with them.

What is the state of the sri?

While teaching machines and the programing concepts they represent are not yet widely used, or even widely available, they have moved from what might be called the laboratory phase into the field-testing phase. There are experiments being carried on throughout the country with relatively large numbers of students in classroom situations.

These experiments cover a wide variety of subject content and extend from the first grade level through college. There have been experiments of the teaching of reading, science concepts and mathematics concepts to very young children. Arithmetic and other subjects have been experimented with in the middle grades, physics and other subjects at the high school level and everything from logic to philosophy at the college level.

In general, the early results are encouraging. With certain subject matters under certain condition, total mastery has been exhibited by most of the experimental student.

Students have reported enjoying the experience of learning with auto-instructional devices. Problems of individual differences seem to be closer to solution. Although many problems remain to be solved, it is already apparent that programed learning for certain objectives with certain kinds of subject matter, is a breakthrough whose dimensions are yet to be assessed. No one, by the way, claims that programed learning will even supplant all other kind of instruction.

Because of the difficulty and expense of devising programed learning, the greatest current lack is in th programs rather than in machines. However, there are sings that this bottleneck may soon be broken. A large educational film producer is now going all-out in a programing effort; several publishers have started or are considering starting one teaching machine manufacturer, sensing the programming problem, began some time ago to develop programs and has several on the market for this fall.

Programs and machines represent a chicken-egg situation at the moment, but there are indications that there may be quite a few chickens and eggs available within the next two years.

The technology of individual instruction and the teacher

If programed learning does become available generally in the near future, what does this mean to the student, the teacher and to education generally?

First, auto-instructional techniques are a promising effort to find a technological solution to the problem of individual differences. Whether a teacher has 35 pupils in five high school classes, he cannot really handle individual differences even through he uses all known human techniques for doing so.

Under present conditions, not teacher can be tutor to each individual student. Teaching machines, properly programed and wisely use, can for certain subject matter and for portions of a school day, provide tutorial experience for individual students. For auto-instruction is tutorial instruction.

From the point of view of the student, this tutorial relationship has other advantages. The student may proceed at his own rate. If he is quick, he is not help us. If he is slower, he is dealing not with a teacher but with a program that has as much time as the student requires and that never tires.

In all cases, the teacher can be relatively sue exactly where the student is which will help in planning other work. And programing of the type described here can institute controls on such things as homework and individual study, which will alleviate problems in connection with other important types of classwork.

Second, any wide-scale introduction of auto-instructional techniques will change the role of the teacher somewhat. It is almost inevitable that the availability of such powerful tools will make the teacher into much more of a professional than he now is.

Any introduction of technology, however, with its accompanying higher professional status will demand more of the teacher in terms of education, experience and professional growth. Teachers will need to understand much more than they do about learning theory and communication; and they will have to exercise sound judgments-in terms, for example, of selecting programs and in determining which educational goals can be best reached through programs instruction and which can be best achieved by other methods.

Further, new types cf instructional systems will evolve as the technology of individual instruction is gradually combined with existing conventional techniques of the classroom and with the mass presentation techniques involving film, television, etc.

This is direction of th future. The machines, the technology, the systems- cured as they are today,improved as they will be tomorrow-will help man become more human if the teachers who will manage them understand instructional technology and make use of it to build teaching into he most human of all professions.

Modern techniques of teaching

Without doubt, the most significant educational development of the next decade will be the increasing application of technology to all parts of the educational system, including teacher education. When examining this statement, however, there is tendency for many educators to think exclusively in terms of machines and to react, therefore, to machine versus human concept.

In thinking through the problem of teacher education and the new technology, the first step that needs to be taken is to understand the term "technology." Technology, as has often been emphasized by students of th field, is much more than machines; technology involves systems; control mechanisms, patterns of organization, and a way of approaching problems. The naive educator who reacts to "machines" when he should be considering technology is a little like a squirrel who chooses to worry about the shell of the nut and pays no attention to the meat. Squirrels are smart enough not to do this.

It might be helpful in this connection to refer to a little-known definition of technology which was stated by Charles Beard many years ago. Beard said.

What then is this technology which constitutes the supremen instrument of modern progress? Although the term is freely employed in current writings, its meaning as actuality and potentiality has never been explored and defined. Indeed, so wide-reaching are its ramifications that the task is difficult and hazardous. Narrowly viewed, technology consists of the totality of existing laboratories, machines, and processes already developed, mastered and in operation. But is far mere objective realities.

Intimately linked in its origin and operation with pure, science, even its most remote mathematical speculations, technology has a philosophy of nature and a method- an attitude toward materials and work-and hence is a subjective force of high tension. It embraces within its scope great constellations of ideas, some explored to apparent limits and others in the form of posed problems and emergent issues dimly understood.

We have been very gradually developing, within education, a technology of instruction. Since I do not have time today to consider all the ramifications of this development, I refer you to a major paper on the subject. Some of the devices developed and put into use during the last 10 years include language laboratories, self-contained audiovisual teaching skits, television, teaching machines of several types and the Corrigan Teletest System. I would like to emphasize once again that these are the symbols of instructional technology-machines-and must be thought of in connection with systems, organizational patterns, utilization practices and so forth, to present a true technological picture.

Considering the entire educational system as a whole, the introduction of audiovisual materials and devices for the purpose of improving instruction was a slow and painful process until the middle 30s. If we would begin to draw a curve at that point, it would look something like. The infusion of money, principally from the Rockefeller Foundation for research in this field, the attention given to instructional technology by a group of very talented men and the availability of better materials and machines all contributed to a rise at that point which did not stop until the beginning of World War II.

As with all educational activities, a slowdown occurred during the war, and the lack of equipment and materials set back the government somewhat. However, the technology of instruction, as everyone knows, moved over into the areas of instructional and military training during the war.

This move relief principally on the previous findings of the educational research and development activities of the 30s and succeed brilliantly by supplying the necessary money and talent for successful implementation. Incidentally, it was during this period that self-instructional devices came to the forefront even though, again as is well known, S.L. Pressey and others had been working on this problem long before.

Following World War II, a great public interest developed in the use of audiovisual materials and during the decade 1945-1955, another upsurge occurred as this technology was introduced into education with some force. Here we must stop to say that of all the levels of education, higher education was the least affected. Oriented to print technology and the lecture system, higher education more or less successfully resisted this movement Since 1955, due to a variety of causes-the application of television, the influence of Ford Foundation projects, the attempts to find solutions to the problems of quality and quantity in education, the curve of instructional technological development has again started up sharply with no leveling-off point in sight in the immediate future. We can now turn to the third perspective-a look at present trends.

The teaching machines movement is merely the latest development in instructional technology that is forcing itself into the educational arena. Actually, we now have a double-pronged technological growth. The first prong is in the field of mass instructional technology and is concerned with those systems, materials and machines suitable for instruction with large groups of people, for the most part as groups. Mass instructional technology includes several types of television, both closed-circuit and broadcast; massed film systems; several types of automatic, programmed projection systems such as the Harwald and Teleprompter units; overhead projection of all types, including the polaroid animated materials; and other equipment.

The other prong consists of technology designed for individual instruction-teaching the individual as an *individual*. Here we come into the area called "teaching machines." Actually, a more general term is necessary. Some prefer to use the term "self-instructional devices", another quite widely used expression is "automated teaching", psychologists are now suggesting" auto-instructional devices."

Skipping, for now, over the problem of terminology and accepting the concept of the technology of individual instruction, which I find very useful, we can list classes of these devices in an ascending order of sophistication from the psycho-technological point of view. They are: (a) individual reading pacers and similar devices; (b) individual viewing and listing equipment for slides, filmstrips, motion pictures, tapes, etc; (c) language laboratories of all types ; (d) specifically programed printed verbal materials such as scrambled textbooks; and (e) teaching machines of the Skinner, Pressey or Crowder types containing carefully worked out verbal or pictorial programs with various ingenious mechanical or electronic arrangements to test student reaction and to inform him of his progress and errors.

These two technologies of mass and individual instruction are under development. The work of A.A. lumsdaine at American Institute for Research, Pittsburgh, Pennsylvania, is one example. In an experiment, Lumsdaine combined instruction with a programed textbook- a form of teaching machine- with the mass use of the Harvey White physics films on television. Over 10 years age, C.R, Carpenter did extensive experimentation at Pennsylvania State University with a "classroom communicator"- a device enabling him to get individual feedback from students while viewing films, listening to lectures and so forth. Dr. Carpenter is at present contemplating new work in this area. The invention and development of the so-called Teletest System by Robert Corrigan and Dean luxton in California is the most sophisticated approach to this problem. This device enables any class receiving television broadcasts to be equipped with individual "teaching machines" which will take silent signals from the TV receiver as to the proper answers to questions and feed them into machines at students' desks so0 that a student, in responding by pushing a button, will receive immediate knowledge of results while, at the same time, a permanent record is made of his performance.

The text step in this procedure -one that is only now being suggested ny a few activities- is illustrated. Here I would like to introduce the concept of instructional systems. Given a technology of mass instruction and a technology of individual instruction, the next step is to combine these two elements on a planned or programmed basis with conventional instructional methods into an instructional system.,

A prototype model of such a system exists in the physics programs for high schools developed at Massachusetts Institute of Technology by the Physical Science Study Committee. After revising the content of the physics course with a new textbook the group has created-or is planning to create: (a) paperback supplementary books, such as the one on soap bubbles; (b) a laboratory manual-with experiments for students(c) a manual on how to build certain apparatus not available from conventional sources; (d) some apparatus; (e) approximately 80 motion pictures; (f) other audiovisual materials such as filmstrips and tapes; and (g) a teacher's manual which is, in effect, a programs for the whole system. Such a system is obviously very costly to create and at least in the eyes of its creators, must be used according to the program laid out for the system.

As I am discussing trends here, the systems concept can be further elaborated. The possibilities of such an idea-an idea which, I think, will inevitably come into being in some parts of our education programs, providing that the emphasis on the quality and survival; values of education in our society continues at its present level or increases. If we consider, for purposes of this discussion, that the instructional process can be broken down discussion, that the instructional process can be broken done into the elements of (a) mass presentation techniques; (b) individual automated teaching; (c) human interaction; (d) individual study; and (e) creative periods, then , in a true instructional technology, these elements would be treated as black boxes in a system. For every instructional problem, assuming the mastery of the technology of each of these elements, the professional teacher and/or curriculum director would create the proper system designed to achieve the agreed-upon objectives.

We have spent some time on the current burst of instructional technology in the form of language laboratories, teaching machines, massed films, and similar developments. And we have examined the trends which take us into the possibilities, at least for some kinds of teaching and learning of the development of instruction systems. Our problem now is to relate this to the specific business of the education of teachers.

It might help in making this connection if we examine the recent past and present status of teacher education in the audiovisual area. Obviously, what is known as audiovisual education is merely another term for instructional technology.

Although there has been some effort at teacher education I audiovisual techniques since the late 20s, the major effort did not begin until after World War II and is by no means completely extended through the teacher education system to this day.

Several patterns have been developed go accomplish the pre-service education of teachers in audiovisual techniques. I commend to your study the January 1959 issues of *Audio-Visual Instruction*, one of the official journals of the Department of Audio-Visual Instruction of the National Education Association. The entire issue is devoted to teacher education and includes excellent statements, not only of various types of programs but also or expected competencies that should come out of such programs.

These patterns, for the most part, hinge upon the concept of "integration"- not in its Mason-dixon Line sense, but in the sense that, theoretically, unless audiovisual materials are integrated throughout a student's experience, he will not be inclined to use them once he becomes a practicing teacher. There are, however, several kinds of integration and also there is a very argument that integration is not the answer.

One pattern, which might be called *complete* integration, assumes that what is needed is the effective and extensive use of audiovisual materials in the entire course experience of the teacher-to-be. This, of course, is based on the old concept which continues a good deal of truth, namely, that teachers tend to teach as they are taught. This pattern assumes that the psychology of audiovisual material usage will be taught in educational psychology, the methods in the methods courses, and so on. Such an organization usually ends up with only the equipment problem relatively untouched and this is usually handled by some sort of compulsory, noncredit laboratory as a pre-or co-request to student teaching. Obviously, there are many places where the ball may be dropped in such a pattern and the only such program I, personally, ever saw which was successful required that the responsible audiovisual professor teach all of these separate units in all of these separate courses. All i can say for that program is that it gave the professor " a lot of mileage" and that he met many interesting people.

A second integration pattern assumes that all that is necessary to know about audiovisual education may be covered in existing methods courses. Here, the crucial factor is the professor. If, as many secondary methods teachers do, he spends a good deal of th course time teaching content, then audiovisual and other things have to go by the board. If he is "hepped" on group dynamics, the same thing can happen. Many elementary methods courses, foe example, spend a good deal of time on the problem of motivation and repeat material which should have been dealt with in educational psychology. The weakness in the methods integration approach is symbolized, I think, by an experience I has some years ago in a major university. A committee of students from a methods course came one day to one of the staff members of the audiovisual center to learn everything about education television because they has to make a report on it the next day in class.

At a few institutions which have rather extensive operating audiovisual centers serving instruction, a third pattern in followed. Here, there is no organized program, but everyone, including professors and students, is involved in projects at the center. Students prepare materials for class reports; professors look up films and preview them for their own courses; everything is one happy audiovisual family among the staff and students, with the only control, when any being the requirement for an operator's card for participation in student teaching.

The fourth pattern the separate course at the pre-service level. Here, following one or more very well-organized textbooks and laboratory manuals on the market, an effort is made to develop the desired competencies on an organized basis. The weakness here, as is probably true in most college courses, can lie in the quality of the instructor and the presence or absence of proper facilities. Some such courses are merely training for equipment jockeys and do not deserve the name of-college-courses. Others are so abstract and impractical as to be without effect. Practice varies. In california, for example, the time devoted to the laboratory phase of such a course runs in different institutions between six and 30 hours in a semester. In the first instance, the laboratory includes only equipment operation, while in the second it covers such items as the preparation of materials and evaluation.

My own preference is for the separate course, but I recognize that institutional differences may govern such decisions. I would put one caveat on the separate course idea. It needs to be combined wit a well-planned program for the use of these materials in student teaching and a general atmosphere of wide use of the audiovisual materials in all the courses in the college.

All of these patterns and all of these institutions we have been discussing are however, conducting teacher education in this field within the pattern of conventional aaudiovisual devices and materials. And our major consideration here today has been that the impact of the new technology will make the audiovisual programs of the 60s a different animal than the conventional "cat" now being regularly "belled " in many institutions. Teaching machines, instructional systems and massed films present nonconventional problems to the teacher-to-be.

The fist generalization we can derive from this fact is, that if the need existed right after World War II to develop al these programs of teacher education in the aaudiovisual field, that need is now presented to you as administrators in a form magnified tenfold- perhaps even 100-fold. Remember, gentlemen, the 22-years old girl you are graduating next June will not be 65 until the year 2004! Some of you in this audience have no conventional audiovisual programs to brag about; others have been content to see their programs drift with the status quo. I suggest that all administrators and faculty members of teacher education institutions ought to start worrying seriously now about their obligations to the school children for the year 2004.

Index